Poe

GW01192024

d

Dreamers

Scríbhneóirí Sliabh Luachra

In conjunction with Kerry Education and Training Board

&

Purple Pumpkin Publishing

First published by

Kerry Education and Training Board

&

Purple Pumpkin Publishing

Dec 2014

A CIP catalogue record for this book

Is available from the British Library

ISBN 978-0-9931412-0-1 Paperback

Poets

&

Dreamers

An anthology of creative writing by the Sliabh Luachra writers group.

Editor: Tommy Frank O'Connor

Assistant Editor: Sharon Fitzpatrick

The contributors. This inspiring writers group has shared a journey, they have supported one another as writers and they are now sharing their works with the wider world. We congratulate them on this publication and we wish them continued success.

The project was funded by Kerry Education and Training Board, under the auspices of the Community Education Programme. The group would like to thank North and East Kerry Development and the (The Kerry Immigrants Group) for their ongoing support to the Project.

SCRÍBHNEÓIRÍ SLIABH LÚACHRA ANTHOLOGY

ACKNOWLEDGEMENTS

Cáit Curtin and Bridie Garvey are the women who ensure the unfussy functioning of our group. Plans can be made in the certain knowledge that everything will be ready at the time and place appointed, whether at our original home in Scartaglin Cultural and Heritage Centre or nowadays in the NEKD Building in Castleisland.

Our founder members were fortunate to attend creative writing workshops in Castleisland Library facilitated by Tommy Frank O'Connor when he was Writer in Residence for County Kerry in 2011. Only a writer of his calibre could see the potential in our initial nervous offerings. Imagine our joy when he later agreed not only to help us set up our own writers group, based in Scartaglin, but also to be our mentor. We have come a long way under his patient tutelage.

We are particularly blessed in Kerry to have Michelle Anne Houlihan, Community Education facilitator with Kerry Education and Training Board. Her knowledge of and enthusiasm for the value of creative writing as a curriculum in lifelong learning is inspiring. She has given us every encouragement and visited us in Scartaglin and Castleisland. Most importantly she has ensured funding for our creative writing courses and for this anthology.

Sharon Fitzpatrick, herself a writer of considerable acumen, founder of Purple Pumpkin Publishing, is our publisher. We are honoured that she has chosen our anthology as her initial publication, and we wish her continuing success.

We wish to thank Patricia Dowling in NEKD for supporting us on this journey. We are thankful to Kate Kennelly and staff at The Kerry Arts Office. Thank you to Award Winning Photographer Billy Horan from Scartaglin, for providing the cover photo. And to Bridie Garvey and Noel Keane for the individual photos of the group.

Our thanks to all of the above and to those who have facilitated our work or the production of this anthology in any way.

SCRÍBHNEÓIRÍ SLIABH LÚACHRA ANTHOLOGY
Editorial
Tommy Frank O'Connor

Inspiration tends to come to those who open themselves to it, as flowers and foliage unfold their leaves and petals to dawn's encouragement. Scríbhneóirí Sliabh Lúachra is a group of writers open to the possibilities of the muse. I am pleased to be mentor to that process. Twenty-four of them have work in this anthology, almost all being published for the first time.

This is the first book from Sharon Fitzpatrick's Purple Pumpkin Publishing, Killarney. What a delightful name! We wish Sharon all the success she deserves. Here we have poems, stories, memoir, essays and recitations from writers at varying stages of development. Some of the pieces have titles in common, based on exercises I have given throughout our workshops in Scartaglin and Castleisland.

The writers vary in age and background. Not all are Sliabh-Lúachra-born but each one has bought into the culture of this heartland. Since Famine times this area has been outward looking. So many people have had to leave to make a living out there in the wider world. Thankfully most never forgot the land that bore them and, through their visits and letters over the decades, have further enriched this ancient culture. Unlike some less confident cultures we have not turned our backs on our past. There's a two-way nurturing through this umbilical cord. We recognise that by embracing it from home or overseas we can better figure out our pathways to the future from the patterns of our past.

We welcome the writers who have settled among us and have brought their enlightenment which contributes to the uniqueness of this work. Writers must understand the importance of a sense of place. We tend to take this for granted but, when we examine why the work of great writers connects with us, we find that their way of getting us to smell their heather, listen to the babble of their brooks and share the thrills and troubles of their heroes/heroines lures into their stories. Our own late, great Con Houlihan

Editorial

was such a master. They also avoid the novice's anxiety to explain everything, allowing us to interpret the work through our senses and emotions.

I commend this group of writers as I hand them over for their new journey within the covers of this book. If you enjoy their work, as I'm sure you will, please let them know.

Since handing over the edited work I've learned of the untimely death of Bridie Callahan, one of our members and a lady of gentle humility and good humour. We will miss her. On behalf of all at SSL I extend our sympathies to Bridie's family and many friends.

Ar dheis Dé ar a anam dílis.

SLIABH LÚACHRA *By Tommy Frank O'Connor*

Just where is this place called Sliabh Lúachra?
The onlooker wanted to know,
When I sang of a homeland of rushes and heather
In an old Boston bar where the world used to go.

You're treating this place as your mother,
As if it had given you life,
And you tell of a masterful violin teacher
Who called his old fiddle — *the wife*!

Can there be such a place in creation
Where the neighbours all gathered to wake
An emigrant's going, as if crossing the Rubicon,
Yet they partied all night to daybreak?

You tell of this *Aisling* or *Vision* —
How old poets like Aodhagán and Eóin Rua
Told murdering tyrants who tried to take Ireland
What innocent blood in time would undo.

How could anyone talk about mountains
As if they were gifted with life?
You even expound of two high purple mounds
Called The Paps — no mere homeland for snipe!

You mention those funny old place-lands —
Like Knightsmountain, Kanturk, Knocknagree,
Gneeveguilla, Kilcummin, a town called Castle Island,
Currow, Cordal and Scart and town-lands like Glounlea.

Sliabh Lúachra

There's no shortage of legends and heroes —
In that reverent way that you mention their names —
And the dew in your eye as you rhyme of the splendour
Of poets and teachers, dance-masters and fiddlers,
Musicians and tailors, and folk who never sought fame
Assures me that this is an enchanted place.

So where **is** your beloved Sliabh Lúachra
Where more people seem happy than sad?
So I lifted my glass and whispered the secret —
It's that Promised Land homing my emigrant heart.

THE WRITERS GROUP

By Bridie Garvey

Here we come, hearts in our hands
The master takes care to calm his new lambs.

Promising never to wound or to harm
He listens well to each story or poem.
He loves to encourage the flair of the scribe,
Suspended in thought, while prodding the hive.

Teas and sultana-fruit scones or cake
Brought in with love by our *Mammy* Cáit.

After tea break we sit satisfied
No worry if our heads feel empty inside.
A topic from Master will get us to think
We blossom the more we are using the ink.

We must have a go with Laptop or pen
To try and develop the writer within.

The master, as always, does what he can
As we all take part in his blessed plan.

The Writers Group

No writer's block here as prose drips from our lips
And poems from our hearts now full of wit.

The bar's higher again, a new deadline looms,
The master's decided we are ready to bloom.

A book or anthology of our good work,
Who knows who might yet like to join in our nook.

A long way to go as he edits our sins
Our Anthology finally ready for print!

THE GREEN GRASS OF IRELAND

By Jimmy Cullinane

Oh green grass of Ireland you feed livestock all,
You grow in the springtime, the summer and fall.
You rest in the winter with temperature low
Beneath hail and frost, the sleet and the snow.

Then you shoot up again, we know it is spring;
The robin and blackbird are starting to sing.
The lambs in the fields cavort ring after ring,
A bed of green grass, what a wonderful thing!

You feed freshly calved cows from out of the stall,
You grow day and night to nourish them all.
They lie down contented, their bellies now full;
The cow with her calf, the heifer and bull.

In moisture and warmth you grow quite a bit,
We then harvest some in a great silage pit.
More we leave grow until late out in May,
Then we mow you and save into sweet bales of hay.

We need you in winter to feed every mouth
When the temperature's low and Jack Frost is about.
We see you in trailers, round or square bales,
Oh green grass of Ireland you're always the best.

The Green Grass of Ireland

You grow in the inch, the valley and the hill,
You've grown there for centuries and always will.
You grow on the dyke, the ditch and the road,
Even up on the thatch of the humble abode.

You grow on the headlands of every field,
You like the soft weather, you give a good yield.
You grow on the golf course, and make a great lawn,
Up on the mountains you are hardy bán.

You feed every creature blessed with a hoof,
And most of the animals up in the zoo.
You feed the small rabbits the frog and the hare;
You feed the young foal and its mother the mare.

Oh green grass of Ireland it's you I adore,
I gaze on your colours from my little half-door.
I will always respect you wherever I go,
The best grazing the world at last coming to know.

The Forgotten Boy   *By Frank Kevins*

In the summer of 1943 Jimmy O Sullivan was an eight-year old boy living in an orphanage in Killarney. He had spent the previous seven months in the care of the nuns who managed the Home as part of the Industrial Schools System, which was prevalent throughout Ireland at that time. He was put there when his mother, Hannah was pregnant with her second child. She was an unmarried single mother, who worked in domestic service on a farm in North Kerry. Her job involved feeding and tending to pigs, and helping with the harvesting of crops.

Jimmy was not aware that his life was about to change greatly. He was standing in line with fifteen other children in an empty room at the orphanage. The Mother Superior entered the room accompanied by an elderly woman, whom she introduced saying "This is Mrs. Murphy, and she wants to take one of you to live with her and her husband on their farm in West Kerry." Mrs. Murphy was aged in her mid-sixties. She wore a dark overcoat with a fox stole on her shoulders. She had a veil attached to her hat, which partially shaded her face.

She walked close to the row of children, and after some deliberation she declared to the head nun "I'll take him," as she pointed at Jimmy. Those three words were to have a profound effect on the young lad for the rest of his childhood. Mrs. Murphy had not heard Jimmy speak, nor did she ask how he felt about being selected in this manner.

Jimmy thought it was terribly cold and ruthless to have been plucked from the nuns by this 'foster mother' as if he was some piece of vegetable or fruit to be picked from a basket. He was fearful of the future and was losing faith in grown-ups, after the way he was treated for the past seven months under the care of the nuns.

The orphanage was run by the sisters in an atmosphere of fear, and totally lacking in affection. They also tried to sever family ties without justification. An example of this was when Jimmy's mum gave birth to his brother John in the District Hospital, the nuns forbade him from going to see his newborn sibling. Jimmy's mother was forced to smuggle him out of the home to visit his brother. She did this while the nuns were at evening prayers. The next time Jimmy saw his brother four decades would have passed. He was always mindful that he was out there somewhere in the world.

A few days had passed since Jimmy was selected to go and live on the farm with the elderly couple, but the paperwork and forms were now ready. He was taken by ambulance to the Murphy's farmhouse, and had mixed feelings about this opportunity to get away from the regime he endured while in the children's home.

Eventually they arrived at the Murphy's residence and were met by Jack Murphy, the husband of the lady who came to the convent. His wife Mary was in the local town doing her shopping.

Once inside the house Jack made tea and gave Jimmy a few slices of homemade bread with it. He then asked the boy to go for a walk with him. Outside the house they met the Murphy's son, John Joe, who worked on the farm, and the only one of the couple's five children living with them.

They walked along the path away from the farm, heading towards the sea. They strolled to The White Strand with its beautiful beaches and roaring sea. Jack explained the ebb and flow of the tide to the young boy. They turned back and made their way home before darkness fell. As they walked back they picked some fuchsias, locally called 'red bells' and sucked the honey from their stamens. They watched a train puffing its way from Caherciveen going towards Renard Point, carrying passengers and goods. The local junior school that Jimmy would be attending could be seen across the fields. He felt confident that his time at this new home would be a good experience.

When they got back to the farmhouse the old lady came forward from the back kitchen, where she had been baking bread. She approached Jimmy and barked loudly "Where were you all evening." The boy replied "I was with him," pointing to the farmer and adding "We went to the White Strand." She picked up a piece of a butter box and gave Jimmy a couple of slaps of it on his head, which knocked him into the corner of the room, and all he could see were sparks and stars. She leaned over the boy and growled "Never go with him again, it is I who signed you out of the convent."

Jimmy's head was still reeling for several minutes, and he wished he was strong enough to defend himself from such beatings. She shouted again at him "I'm the boss of this house and what I say goes. Now get out to the barn and get some straw to make your bed." This was something new for the lad to learn to do.

He had to get sewn mail bags and fill them with straw to make a mattress for his bed.

He was shown to his room dragging his mattress after him. Mrs. Murphy's parting words to Jimmy that night were "Tomorrow you will be shown how to milk cows." It soon dawned on the boy that he would be sharing a room with the old man. He was not too worried because Jack appeared to be a kind sort of a man. But for an eight year old to share a bedroom with a sixty five year old man who was no relation of his, would take a bit of getting used to.

The battle lines were now being drawn, and his broad shoulders for one so young, would be tested to their limit, if he was not to buckle under the pressure he would be subjected to over the next eight years.

A Sunny Glade

By Cáit Curtin

As I linger here on the river bank, recalling days gone by,
Pictures of my childhood days drift slowly through my mind:
Days spent beside this river, watching fish swim by;
The little damson and brown trout that leaped to catch the flies.

The sun so gentle on my head was like a loving touch,
Feet resting on the river stone, the cooling water's rush.
I listened to the silence, then heard the cuckoo's call,
Bees buzzing in the foxgloves, young boys playing ball.

Other memories take me back, which causes me to smile
When I picnicked with my children, how great was their delight!
We had sandwiches and apples, currant tops and lemonade;
It was our little piece of Heaven, this green and sunny glade.

It was there the cattle came to drink, sheep and horses too,
And in the shrubs the hare would sit, so still and out of view.
The pheasant and the rabbit, the otter sleek and black,
The vixen fox and frisky cubs, sometimes a water rat.

A Sunny Glade

Observing all this taught the children great respect
For all the things of nature, how to care and do their best.
They knew each creature had its place in nature's plan of life
So happy in their little world where everything's alive.

I look around and see the scenery has changed,
This one-time, lovely sunny glade looks so sad and strange:
The waters are a murky brown, the wild life now all gone;
The river bank is overgrown, with briars and yellow gorse.

Still! I hold my memories and when it's cold and damp
I remember all those golden days down by the river bank.
It's where I go to soothe my soul and find great peace of mind,
That river bank of long ago when I was just a child.

MY FAVOURITE HOLIDAY
By Anna Brosnan

Choosing my favourite place has proved a difficult assignment. There is a big wide world to choose from, but alas I can only choose from my limited experience. I envy people when I hear them say — "I travelled the world." What a privilege!! I remember reading an interview which Jill Ireland the famous actress gave when she was dying from Cancer. With great sadness she said, — "I hate the thought of leaving this beautiful world."

The places that have left a lasting impression on me are Niagara Falls and Pinang in Malaysia. The sheer majesty and the mighty roar of the falls has not dimmed with the passing of time, but again and again I find myself reliving the peace, tranquillity and the diversity that is Malaysia. Malaysia was a British colony and known as Malaya until 1957 when it became an independent Country. Malays form the majority of the population but there are sizeable Chinese and Indian communities. There are many languages though most people speak some English. Islam is the official religion but there are others such as Hindu and Catholic also.

Though I have spent some time in many parts of Malaysia including Malacca and the Capital Kuala Lumpur, my favourite place is Pinang. Pinang is an island connected to the mainland by a 13-mile bridge, because of its natural beauty it is known as the pearl of the Orient.

I was first spellbound by its spectacular sunsets and the speed with which it enveloped the long low extended horizon. I would stand on my balcony, in my upstairs bedroom, and gaze enraptured at the breath-taking landscape as the low hanging sky changed colour, becoming a blazing ball of fire sprinkled with a golden hue: the gentle sea breeze lancing the humidity; the smell of the rain on the ground as it evaporated and disappeared; the birds twittering on the palms trees; the distant hum of traffic, and the child minder taking Kinsley for a late walk around the garden before bed time. My mind and soul at peace in perfect harmony with the universe. When I ponder on those times now I am reminded that — 'For one brief shining moment, once there was a Camelot.'

My Favourite Holiday

The Malaysian way of life is very different. Regardless of how poor people are, they can afford to eat out. The sidewalks are like open-air restaurants: tables and chairs arranged everywhere; always crowded with people, and the crackling sound of numerous dialects and languages, the air heavy with the aroma of spicy foods. There are five-star hotels and modest restaurants to cater for all strands of society. I have fond memories of dinner one evening in the Shangri-La Hotel as we enjoyed our gourmet eastern meal: musicians serenaded us with western music. On leaving we took the rear exit leading to the golden sands and the gentle lapping of the warm ocean. There on the beach two artists stood selling their paintings though it was approaching midnight. Heaven and earth seemed united under a star-lit sky.

During my times in Malaysia I have climbed Pinang Hill and visited one of its biggest Buddhist temples. On entering we had to remove our sandals and I think we were expected to kneel and pray in front of the golden statue of Buda, as it held court surrounded by various images and a cluster of candles emitting a strong aroma of perfumed wax. I shied away from kneeling in prayer and walked on.

There are so many unique places to see in Pinang. There is a spectacular tropical Butterfly farm and insect preservation that looks like a bed of multi-coloured pansies in flight. The habitat of thick foliage and rare plants is constantly sprayed with a heavy mist.

Malaysia with its abundance of spectacular beaches; its luxurious hotels; its historical buildings; its hawkers, and its sky-scraper shopping arcades all blending together in harmony is a land of dreams. Yet with all its vibrancy, colour and contradictions this eastern paradise can sometimes induce a restless loneliness and a longing for my own place. This is why I will always remain anchored in Tullig. The ties that bind me are unbreakable but that is a story for another time.

OVER THERE IN COUNTY CLARE

By James Flynn

Over there in County Clare there lives a jolly lass.

She's Norma May and works each day by selling coal and gas.

She met a man for a black and tan one night in Brogan's bar,

She got home drunk and like a punk she even drove her car.

Her face was red she went to bed that evening after ten,

She got up late in quite a state and drank a glass of gin.

She went to town and like a clown, inside in Garvey's shop,

She beat a man with a frying pan, and no one shouted stop.

She had a cat his name was Batt, She'd feed him nuts and pandy,

But being nice at half the price, she <u>fed him milk with brandy.</u>

EASTER —TIME FOR RENEWAL

By Hanna O' Sullivan

I love this time of year.

It is a happy time, a time of promise.

The days are stretching out and getting warmer.

Awakening to birdsong, I find it uplifting to see the calves jumping around in the fields; drowsy cows chewing the cud; early butterflies fluttering in the reality of their new world.

It is also a time of inner renewal, time to look deep in the soul and see what needs tending and mending; time to weed out and plant anew.

It is time to sweep out the dust and cobwebs, and allow the sunshine in.

Happiness is an inside job.

The soul needs joy to flourish.

Invite joy into your life, tend it with care and love and enjoy its blossoming.

The Spider's Web

By Noel Keane

Macro silk thread, spider spun,
Outward spokes, like rays of sun,
Inward spiral, neatly laid,
Lethal trap for insects made.

Trampoline-like from on high,
Unsuspecting to a fly,
Spider, patient, very still,
Calmly waiting for the kill.

Hours go by and ne'er a stir,
'Til concentration wanes to blur,
An un-intending lapse, and then,
The spider's next, entwined within.

FATE
By
Anne Coffey

Michael Schumacher is struggling to cope with his horrific accident. He crashed while skiing on the slopes of Meribel. Banged his head off a rock and his helmet broke in two. It was there he met his fate. He had major surgery and is now in an induced coma.

The seven times world champion was a speed addict even on the slopes of the French Alps. Married with two children, they are now by his bedside. Michael Schumacher had ninety two wins in his formula one career and won five world titles for Ferrari. A pure genius.

His father bought him a bicycle and he went on the course with it. Then he drove on the track and won all around him. He is now a multi-millionaire. I hope he returns to good health and continues to enjoy his retirement because this sporting legend deserves it.

FLIGHT
By Patricia Horgan

I've said my good byes, I've taken flight,
I rise up like a soaring kite.
Without any luggage I travel light,
Not a compass or sat-nav in sight.
Dressed in steel blue with a pale buff,
With climate change I've had enough.
I look ahead to brighter days,
Of scorching sun and burning rays.

I see fields of green, gold and brown,
Like an earthly patchwork of eiderdown;
Boreens gilded with whitethorns,
And busy streets with blaring horns;
The high stone cross of the church steeple,
And the congregating of the people.

Soon I will leave behind the land
And trade it for sea, sun and sand;
The soft waves as they caress the beach,
And listen as the children screech.
Golden sand dunes standing tall,
Soon Mother Nature will fell them all.

Flight

I see varying hues of blue and green.
I wonder how long it has been
Since I left home for my *Vacances*.
I must descend for to refuel,
I need to hydrate to keep cool;
Tall ships resting by the shore
And fishing vessels by the score.

Her I am at my destination
Surely you've guessed it,
I'm a swallow in migration.

The Reek

By Marian Pender

Seven a.m. and already it's bustling, upwards mainly. By seven p.m., the trend will be reversed; the babble muted, the breathing heavier. There will be more audible grunting, more silent communication. The finishers will have sore feet, tired muscles and contentment.

The hill, with its disingenuous gentleness has an insistent incline leading to the mountain and its spectacular summit. It changes little from season to season, or year to year, its vegetation being heather and wild grasses. Both struggle to maintain roots in soil loosened by trampling feet, and rolling scree dislodged by the stout sticks of ash. Pilgrims are not always the most reverent of people.

A scar has developed over centuries on this hill. Compacted earth, a path almost, it twists and climbs, guiding those who follow it around boulders and marshy patches to higher ground. At the lip of the ocean, the hillside is the home place of soft drizzle, and it doesn't take crowded jostling to lose footing here.

Norah is already a few hundred feet up; but off the path, to the right, where a small camouflage shelter protects her somewhat as she unpacks her picnic and settles down with her gear. It's said to have been a place of pilgrimage for over 5000 years; this is her fifth. She observes the steady stream of people on the ascent; their colour and movement temporarily changing the face of the hillside. She smiles smugly knowing conditions are just right for her and reaches for her rucksack. The first difficult turn is just 20 minutes up and those who haven't yet purchased an ash stick for support will slip, and fall, spectacularly.

And Norah is ready to capture them; for Monday's tabloids.

FUNERAL

By Lorraine Carey

I sat with my children
Two rows down from the draped coffin.
The heady sweetness of incense, like cooled molasses,
Returned me floating into a different church —
St. Mary's now a memory.

Tears stumbled down reticent cheeks,
My solitary tissue sodden.
Squashed into a little fake brain,
Fist moulded and nestled.
Trying to focus on the beamed ceiling,
And on the white robed man's words.

I drifted onto a wall plaque.
Poring over and over
The chiselled details, a futile distraction.
Tilting my head, aiming to cry in reverse
But my stubborn ducts were not accepting.

Funeral

Hallowed hymns freeing swallowed sadness.
A smiling photo standing on the oblong box.
This boxed body, oblivious to the ceremony,
Unfolding like a bud on fast forward.
My lap, cold and damp with tears
for you,
who haven't died yet.

What to do about…………………… ?

By Sharon Fitzpatrick

Excuses, excuses, excuses, any excuse not to take a lunch.

"The fruit is bruised, when I take it out my bag." I give her a lunch box.

"The lunch box won't fit in my school bag." I suggest carrying it.

"It's too awkward; I have enough stuff to carry." I offer to carry her art stuff for her.

"No way, I can carry it myself." Problem solved, I told her I will drop in some sandwiches and leave them in the school office.

"I don't like sandwiches, they're boring." That's easy; I will get her a wrap, with spicy chicken and cheese.

"They are too smelly, and it's embarrassing being called to the office." I could arrange for them not to call her. She could just go at the start of lunch to get it. But that wasn't good enough. I offered to bring in some homemade soup and leave it in the canteen.

"I am not heating anything in the microwave; there is always a big queue."

Things got even worse. She started at breakfast time too.

"I don't like Bran flakes anymore." I gave her alternative cereals that I knew she liked. But she didn't like them anymore. I offered to make her toast.

"I don't like white bread anymore." I bought brown bread. She ate it for a few days.

What to do about................... ?

"Brown bread has no taste; I am fed up eating it. It's boring." I got some lovely soda bread. She loved it. Finally getting somewhere, until......

"Mum, don't get me soda bread anymore; I am sick of having the same thing." My patience was wearing thinner and thinner. What am I going to do about her? Next day I said to her to have some fruit, she took one very small orange. On asking her to eat another one, I got another excuse.

"They weren't that nice."

It progressed to dinner times. Watching everything I did when cooking. Wanting to dish out the dinners and plating a smaller portion of potatoes for her-self. Not knowing what to do about her, I asked the Doctor for advice. The Doctor confirmed she had an eating disorder, and I had to persuade her to come and see her. And so the long process of recovery, I hope will start.

BULLY

By Patricia Horgan

When I think back on my young days
In the old school yard,
Were it filmed history, well
You might have starred.

I often wonder if you knew
The pain and hurt you caused,
If only for one minute
You stood back and paused.

You shredded my young confidence,
Moral was oh so low;
My back to the wall
I had no place to go.

I could never understand
Why we could not be friends,
For I have since then learned
That life has many bends.

But I have moved on with my life
And left it all behind.
The one big morale in this poem
Is — to everyone be kind.

ACCIDENTAL ADVENTURE

By Elsie McDonald

Lunches packed in saddlebags, the boys sped off towards the woods.

"Which track will we follow this week?" shouted Len. "To the left, to the left," came the reply in the nick of time before Arthur missed the turning.

There were a few screeching stops for Chris to fill his pockets with interesting objects on the way. Arthur the leader kept up the pace, dodging boulders and tree roots that would tip them over the handlebars. Len skilfully jumped his bike over the little brook and Chris, the collector, called out from the tail, "Wait for me." He eventually managed to catch up when the trail became too overgrown to ride. The boys dismounted and Hayden the hungry said, "Great. Is it time to eat?" "No" yelled the others as they parked their bikes against a rather large oak tree. All four ran off down the narrowing path to explore.

They hadn't gone far when Arthur suddenly dropped out of sight. "Stop playing about," Len scolded. "He's disappeared down that hole," observed Chris.

While they were wondering what they should do, Arthur was spinning down and down, twisting and turning, feet up, then feet down. As he tumbled he thought, "This is going to hurt" but to his surprise and great relief, he reached the bottom with a splash.

"Are you alright Arthur?" The startled boys shouted down the hole. Arthur didn't answer but they knew he was alright; they could hear his laughter echoing up. Not wanting to miss out, Len, Chris and Hayden joined hands to form a circle and after one, two, three, they jumped into the hole. Down they went round and round, deeper and deeper until they too landed with a huge splash.

The four had discovered a bright new world; it was a huge cavern with what looked like crystal chandeliers hanging from a high domed ceiling. There were twisted vines trailing down and Len the Lion-heart couldn't resist grabbing hold of one and swinging like Tarzan. As he spun out of control he crashed into one of the chandeliers before dropping back into the stream. The boys clapped with joy: they hadn't enjoyed themselves this much before.

They stepped out of the water on to the greenest, softest mossy grass that smelled so fresh and felt like bouncy cushions. It formed great mounds. They ran to the top like excited puppies and rolled back down, splashing into the water, laughing as they had never laughed before.

Out of breath, they stopped to rest. They sat beside a strange looking bush; it had bright green leaves and the biggest red berries. The sight was too much for Hayden the hungry. "Do you think we can eat them?" he asked "You try one and if you fall down dead, we won't," laughed Len. Hayden thought about it for a while. They looked so good, he tried a tiny piece. "It tastes like strawberries and cream," he said and popped the rest into his mouth. "Ohhh, Ohhh, he groaned and held his tummy and fell backwards. Arthur and Len looked worried, but Hayden started giggling, "Only Joking; Gotcha."

The water that had cushioned their fall was bright and glistening like champagne and meandered as far as they could see. It teemed with strange little fish; they followed them as they danced downstream until their backs ached with bending. The stream opened up into a beautiful blue lagoon, where the boys swam, the fish tickled their legs as they brushed past. Flying above them was a flock of magnificent birds; they were bright red, with golden beaks and the deepest of blue trails hanging from their tail feathers. Their song was hypnotic and the sound danced around the chambers like a lullaby.

They seemed to have been exploring for hours, enjoying all the sights and sounds of this strange place. It was Hayden's hunger that alerted the gang to thoughts of going home, but how would they get out? "We had better find a way out," Arthur said.

In that instant a gigantic wind swirled around them, lifting them off their feet spinning them round and round, up and up, spewing them out. They landed on the ground with a thump. Four dizzy and puzzled lads arrived back in the woods by the big old tree where they had left their bicycles.

They searched for the hole but it was nowhere to be found. Was it a dream? They pinched themselves in disbelief.

Searching for answers, Chris the collector emptied his pockets and there in his pile of treasure was — you guessed it, a tiny shard of chandelier.

WOODLAND WALK
By Judith Carmody

As we stroll through grassy woodlands,
Warm evening light speckling through,
Your loving transports me to a trance,
My heart waltzing to our special dance.

My hand in your hand I feel entwined
Kicking through the leaves like turning pages
So many moments, days, so many ages
Together we've weaved through life's maze.

As dusk wraps it blanket around us, I smile.
I look with affection, and your smile mirrors mine.
One direction, one thought, one special bond;
Locked in a moment, to be forever fond.

Garlands of flowers affirm our unity;
The magic, mystic, the earthy beauty.
All movement like a river with gentle entity,
As moonlight beams on this serenity.

WHISPERS *By Donna McSweeney*

"Every blade of grass has its Angel that bends over it and whispers, 'grow, grow'" *The Talmud.*

Waiting is what she does now. She waits for visitors, tests and she waits to die. She is also waiting for something else. Something she doesn't know she is waiting for.

We've all had to wait, at times. Some patiently. Some not so much. We've waited to pay for groceries. We've waited to see the doctor. It takes one minute to see if the stick turns pink. It takes years of hard work to retire comfortably. Waiting of this kind though, is perhaps the biggest test of all. She asks herself if she is ready to go, to leave her family. Are they ready? Maybe she shouldn't be thinking these things. Maybe she will be healed.

We all die. Some view death as an escape. Whether it be from pain or from loss of hope. Death is not even a thought for some, like the teenager struck by a car as he walks home from school. It can be painful or painless. She is suffering. Yes, her body is failing, but it is her inability to touch that is most hurtful. She cannot embrace her family. She wonders will she ever make love again. When the time comes, when the doctor can do no more, will she have the strength to cuddle her children? Do they know how painful it is to leave them?

As she waits, a child comes to her. She's seen this child before. A little girl that roams the halls, bringing a bit of cheer to the patients. She knows she should tell her to leave but she hasn't seen a soul other than doctors and nurses all day. As the girl nears, she sees her face is no longer puffy, but thin now, almost gaunt. They've stopped her medication. With a smile, the little girl tells her it is her time, her time to become an angel. The women imagines her with little fairy wings and manages a weak smile.

Then, she crawls into the bed, places her hand in the woman's and lays her head on her chest. They lay there, peacefully until she realizes how much she loves this little girl. Tears roll down her cheeks. How could this be happening? This little girl has so much ahead of her. If it were possible, she would change places with her. But she has so much to do too.

Slowly they drift off. Not to sleep, but to another place in their minds. Places where things are different. Where they are not sick. Unknown to each other, their thoughts are nearly much the same. They are playing in tall grass with members of their families. Playing and having fun is what they dream of.

Their breathing stops. Then their hearts. Nurses race in with a crash cart. The little girl, being a surprise in the isolation room, is carried away to another crash cart. But not before she gained her wings and performed her first act as an angel.

After much effort, the woman's heart starts beating again. The angel was worried, but the nurses and doctors were able to do their jobs effectively. Knowing that all would be fine, she leaves, reluctantly, for there are others deserving a kiss from an angel.

As time moves forward, the woman's progress amazes doctors. She is free from this malignancy that was killing her. Life has changed for her. It has a new meaning, a new feel to it. She will never take it for granted and she knows how fortunate she was to have met this little girl, the angel who saved her life. It will never be forgotten, what they shared, what they had in common. She hopes, when it is her time, she has the opportunity to earn her wings. For now, she makes her hospital dreams a reality; she embraces her family. They go for long walks, in the tall grass, hearing the whispers.

REMEMBERING PATRICK O'KEEFFE
By Jimmy Cullinane

Today we recall a Fiddler of fame,
Who lived in Glounthane, O'Keeffe was his name;
He is dead fifty years now, but we still hear him play
He is interred in Killmurray beneath the red clay.

It was the year sixty-three that we got a hard frost,
Sure that was the time that poor Patrick was lost;
He died in the hospital, St Catherine's Tralee,
He had the finest funeral that you'd wish to see.

He roved through the countryside day after day
Teaching the young and the old how to play;
He taught many pupils, was generous and giving,
At a half crown a tune he earned his living.

He played at all dances and American wakes.
He played in Killarney the town by the lakes;
At station-mass parties all night he would toil,
When the porter got slack, he would call for more oil.

He composed many tunes, he had a great brain,
He would play all night long in moonlight or rain.
He gave them his music, it was all in his head;
They wrote it all down with a sharp pencil lead.
They went to Scartaglin for a drink in a pub
And had many a great party with music and grub.

Remembering Patrick

Seamus Ennis he came with the pipes on his knee,
He went into Charlie Horan's to tape fiddlers three:
Julia Clifford, Denis Murphy and Patrick all played —
It was there that the record *Kerry Fiddlers* was made

He got a lift from a priest as he hitched into town,
Do you go to mass Patrick? He was serious and sour;
One hour in a church, father is like a wet day,
A day playing my Fiddle seems just like an hour

O'Keeffe was humorous witty and wise
With a fine head of hair and two roving eyes.
A monument to Patrick has been erected in Scart
Sculpted by Mike Kenny, that genius of Art.

Patrick's past pupil are now getting scarce,
One after the other they have run their last race;
They have handed his music down to the young
A legacy to treasure for generations to come.

THE STATION *By Madeline O' Connor*

In rural Ireland the Station was a very important occasion in any parish. Each family in a town land hosted the Station in their turn. It was a stressful time for many, as people were worried about having the house ready and everything in place for the occasion.

Many people lived in old farmhouses with thatched roofs which needed to be repaired. The straw or rushes had to be prepared and the scallops made to fasten the thatch. The chimney had to be cleaned down and the crane cleaned of soot. The good delph was taken out and if anything was missing it could always be borrowed; in fact the same teapot was known to appear at every station in the locality.

On the morning of the station everybody was up early as the milking had to be done and the open fire started in the kitchen. When the priest arrived he heard confessions in the room. People were sometimes a little nervous approaching him, especially if they hadn't been for a while, or had something special on their minds.

While confessions were in progress the parish clerk, who always accompanied the priest, converted the kitchen table to an altar. It was lifted on to two kitchen chairs .A gallon of water was placed beside it and some salt .Before Mass began the priest blessed the holy water and everybody took some home afterwards. After Mass the station dues were collected each householder's name was called in their turn. While this was going on the women were rushing around boiling kettles and putting eggs on to boil for breakfast. A number of men were selected to dine with the priest, preferably those with some idea of table manners.

The breakfast consisted of homemade brown bread and boiled eggs with a selection of other cakes and scones. A desert of jelly and custard was served after. In later years the menu changed and turkey and ham and salad was served.

The priest left immediately after breakfast and everybody relaxed. It was then the bottle was uncorked and maybe a few bottles of Guinness were passed around. As children we loved the day of the station; we had nice things to eat for days afterwards.

Place

By Rose Riordan

I remember as a child my mother, my brother Paddy, my sister Paula and I went to Kilkee, a seaside resort in Co Clare, for a week's holiday every year. It was such a happy time in my childhood. We went down on a bus. That was a big treat, as we always walked to school, and to town. We stayed in a B&B called Keane's. That was our surname too, even though we had no connection with them; that's how I can still remember the B&B name. We had beautiful bedrooms with snow white sheets and lovely quilt covers on the bed. Everything was so neat and clean, with pink tablecloths on the tables when we went down for breakfast. Our breakfast was served up to us, fresh orange juice and a fry every morning. And the aroma of a fried breakfast every morning was wonderful, as our breakfast at home was nearly always porridge. I always remember when we arrived in Kilkee the beautiful scent of burning turf and the smell of the sea. I loved that smell. Even to this day those sensory treats still greet the nostrils; I still love it. People still burn turf; I have visited other seaside resorts and never found that beautiful smell.

My mother used to let us go to the cinema most nights, and she would go to the bingo. We would meet her in the bingo hall after the film-show was over, and then go back to the B&B. That was a great treat for us children; we really enjoyed going to the cinema — and being beside the bingo hall. They were very happy times, as we would sit on the beach most days and then go swimming. We saw the beach for that week only, as we lived in a city. And as my mam was a very busy woman we had her all to ourselves for that precious time. I have so many happy memories as I look back now. Everything that week was so wonderful, it's hard to put into words. How happy we all were to be away on our holidays, and the wonderful time we had with my Mam. We all hated coming home.

Writing this story has stirred up so many wonderful memories. The scents and smells of burning turf and of the sea, the bus trip down, and the wonderful place we stayed in. And the lovely time we had with my Mam, and the delicious food we had every day. The swimming in the sea, and all the other treats Mam brought us, especially ice-cream. I really enjoyed going down memory lane, the time I spent in Kilkee was a great treat.

MY FAVOURITE PLACE   *By Ann Kiely*

It is nice to have a sense of place as the saying goes. 'You can take the Irish Man out of the bog but you cannot take the bog from his inner being.' No matter where you go in the World, we seem to recognize the features of a person from the Emerald Isle, which can be comforting in a distant land far from home.

Sometimes we look at life through rose tinted glasses from those far days, when the sun was always shining and the days never seemed to end. But there are always ups and downs, and we have to manoeuvre around them, and see brighter days ahead.

For me it is nice to go back to my youth before the Industrial and Technology era took over, and to look at life from a different perspective. The modern conveniences have brought a lot of comfort to people. No more taking the bucket and walking a mile to the well. A big change when it was piped to the house and at a turn of a tap we had water. We did a lot of cooking in the open fire. I remember the big black saucepan well for cooking the bacon and cabbage. I was not happy if I was made to sit down and turn the wheel of the bellows which gave wind under floor through a pipe to the fire.

But those times had their pluses and minuses. My brother Paul was very particular about his white shirts and there would be war if any soot got on them, which of course it sometimes did.

I would tell him, if he did not shut up I would burn them. All hell would break lose then.

The older generation then had a more relaxed attitude to life, not as stressed as we are now. No clinics to chill out in. Instead we went visiting the neighbours and that took our mind off our problems for now.

My Favourite Place

It is great to visit one's home place. For me the road leading past the house has not changed at all. There is still grass growing in the middle of the road and there is hardly any new houses built there. Eighty years; so little has changed. My late Father told me a long time ago that it was the Main road to Dublin. I had to smile as I regard it as a boreen nowadays. The tourist board have taken it over and it is a place to walk for the Visitors and the Walking groups. It is called the Golden mile where people can walk in safety and a beautiful walk it is too.

We have a fantastic view of the countryside. Overlooking Knockfierna the fairy hill, where the locals have opened a cottage and they hold a rambling house there once a month with song and dance and story-telling. It is great to keep our unique heritage alive and it is a great way for people to meet.

Forty miles away we had fantastic views of Shannon Airport. The big Bird taking off and landing. The family could be sitting down eating their lunch and they would hear the plane outside and we all would run out to have a good look. These memories seem hilarious to look back on. We were so innocent then, which it should be — all before we would face the stresses and strains of modern life.

Long ago we did not get to the local town very often. Our mode of transport was a pony and trap and that was to take us to Mass once a week. I remember going to a relation's funeral and in those days the earth was put on top of the coffin. Then, a man named Beery O'Donnell, because of his love of the black stuff, was shovelling the clay and he was so drunk that he fell in on top of the coffin and had to be pulled out. We had tears of laughter that day, but the priest was not impressed. Memories are precious.

Postscript; if age could; if Youth knew

MOTHERHOOD

By Patrick O' Connor

Dear Mother Earth,
We have come a long way,
A product of your oceans
That time cannot decay.

Ethiopian Lucy changed
Her daughter's ways,
To evolve, adapt, evolve
To whom we are today.

Mother Mary, Mother to us all,
With your blessing and understanding
Will help us when we fall.

I pray and thank my mother,
Who had to go away,
For the strength, resolve and kindness
You taught me day by day.

Mother's day is Sunday,
So boys don't be too small;
Give with Love and Loyalty,
A day of proud recall.

Dan Got A Chimney   *By Sukie Mac*

As I bent down, once again, building another stook I cursed my husband's absence. Freaking turf, it was hard work with him those few years but all this bending and stretching in the dry wind on the top bog was vile without him. I'll get this row done and go see how the bog tea is brewing; three hours of this back-breaking toil calls for that special tea. Mmm! It's like the milk and honey of the Promised Land. Oh Dan, how I miss you, especially now.

His words ran through my mind like a rural rule book; "Girl, a fierce day at the bog, saw young Jerry Pa, what a scoundrel! His father, a great man, will be reeling in his grave. His turf'll be wet and heavy that's for sure; won't draw fire either. You should've seen him, the cocky little sod. No turning or footing, throwing up a giant stook at the edge of the bank like one of them sculptures on the side of the good road. Tis no way to treat the sods. Ye have to give turf its time, turn it, and leave it to dry in the wind for at least two weeks, then foot it."

"What's a foot Dan?"

I was a naïve city girl, civilised, used to imported Polish smokeless coal. We were just married, Dan had said not to go up to the bog this first year because the midges would know I was a wee blow-in, but each evening he brought home all the news from up above. 'Til he met me, well no, 'til we started courting, as he put it, Dan was a thirty- five-year member of the bachelor club. Never had time, so he said, for the girls in the village; then they all got themselves married or moved away — not that he was too worried about that.

According to village gossip I was a flighty piece from the city, twenty two years in my cotton socks. The old men had me pegged as a gold-digger, only in it for Dan's cash, they warned him.

If they only knew how we met! Six years before our wedding I was actively running away from home. I was a bit messed up, sitting on the train, no clear plan, just to get away. Dan sat down opposite. The train lurched to a stop. We bumped heads and in the ensuing apologies we got into conversation. He chatted to me like I was a person, not like mam always treating me like a child. Told me all about his trip to the city to see a solicitor. He was chuffed to bits because Auntie Cissie had left him a few acres and a cottage with a chimney.

"Don't all houses have chimneys?" I giggled

"Ah, in the city you probably get them without don't you? Those on the gas, or electric? In the country it means you have a wee bit of bog. Each bog was split up and if you had a house in the area on the day they split, you got a strip of bog. The saying goes 'the bank goes with the chimney'. New houses don't get banks."

He told me about his Auntie Cissie and her south-east facing bank of turf, her couple of acres of mature trees and her house built after the big war when Uncle Peter came home. Peter was never the same. He sat in his room all day; at night he suffered horrific nightmares. They lived a quiet, simple life with Cissie providing for them, taking in washing and cleaning the big house. Dan said that nowadays Peter would get counselling for the atrocities he had seen in the war.

Cissie was the only one who knew that Dan painted. He'd wanted to go to college, but there was no money and he daren't have told his daddy. So he got work as a carpet fitter in the nearby town and began to paint in Cissie's attic.

The train started again. We shared our food and in a very serious voice Dan asked for my address, not my phone number, not that I would've given an old man my phone number. He just asked for my address. I felt so grown up writing out: 13 Poplar Crescent, Mayfield, Cork. He folded the paper and put it in his wallet, from which he took a fiver. He advised me to go home. If you don't go home you won't get my letter, he said. The thought of receiving his letter won my agreement.

He wrote, it arrived two weeks later, full of news from his new house, of his plans. He asked my opinion on colours, and a bunch of questions about school and home. I wrote straight back telling him all the gossip from school, tales about our Darro, my little troublesome brother, Mammy and her hips and Daddy and his whippets. I told him of how I hated school and of my love for Nana who died earlier that year. After filling four pages from my jotter I wrote — write back soon.

Dan began suggested careers, courses, subjects. We wrote to each other by return, never letting a week go without a letter dropping on either mat. Without realising it, my attitude to school became more positive. I did okay in my Leaving Certificate Examination and got a place at the Institute of Technology doing business. He began to come up to Cork on the odd Saturday. We'd have lunch in the old Roche's Stores, then off to the pictures on Grand Parade. On fine days we went for long walks by the Lee out to the Carrigrohane Straight.

He was made redundant. Wooden floors came into fashion; there was little call for carpets and prospects of another job were poor. Auntie Cissie's house was now his passion. Each visit brought tales of windows, loft conversions and insulation, thanks to his savings and redundancy package. In his descriptions I could almost see the cottage; one long hallway with the rooms off it on both sides. On the left was a den, a single bedroom and the master. On the right was a small kitchen with a new extension housing a scullery and utility room. The bathroom and study came next, then another single bedroom.

The loft extension was Dan's studio. His painting was still hidden from the world but now he had more space to explore his artistic streak. Outside, he crafted raised beds to grow vegetables, fruit bushes and trees. Chickens, ducks and a bad tempered goose had been joined recently by a female goat.

On my nineteenth birthday Dan arrived in his new acquisition, an old Renault 4 van. We ate in a Chinese Restaurant and over coffee Dan put a small jewellery box in front of me.

"Lilian, will ye marry me?"

"I don't know, yes, no, yes, I think, I mean we haven't even kissed."

He smiled shyly and suggested we take care of that straight away. Of course I knew Dan was the man for me, I had always known.

I drank the bog tea, I cried again and then got back to my wee stooks. Young Daniel or Danielle in my belly keeps me going; my new future, but oh how I miss my Dan.

I thought back to the removal and funeral. People, friends in their throngs came to pay their respects. Grief receded a little in the tender love of Dan's extended family. I showed his sister some of his paintings. She cried because she never knew he was so talented. I gave her the one of weeping willow by the stream. She then got the gallery involved, and I am glad she did. Last week I sold the second of his paintings; now they want to put on an exhibition.

"Dan, it's what you always wanted, love; you'll be remembered as an artist not the auld man with the snip of a wife."

Stooks done, fire out. Jerry Pa came over and offered to draw it home in a couple of weeks. So if the weather holds the shed will be full for the winter.

"Just in time for our baby, Dan."

The doctor said there was nothing that could've been done. He had a massive stroke, he told me, and it was better for him that he died. It was small comfort. I would've been the best nurse to him. Dan died without knowing about the baby. Wherever he is I know this news is what makes our marriage complete. Mammy is coming down for the last few weeks to help out. She is getting to be a right country yoke, loves getting the eggs in the morning and weeds the beds like she was born to it. Patting my tummy as the wee one kicks,

"Sure oh sure we'll be alright, little one."

I smile and wipe away a proud tear. An improvement, Dan would say.

THE VILLAGE
By Noel Keane

Oh! but to live in a village of yore,
A fabric of life, long gone before.
Of leisurely pace, no stress to endure,
Wealth of good neighbours, friendship secure.

To rise in the morn, to rooster's loud crow,
And salute the old milkman, his face all aglow,
The click of his horse hooves on cobblestone way,
"Thank God" be his blessing "for this heavenly day."

A stroll up the street, would be special as well,
No motorised hoot, just the ring of a bell.
Peg Nolan all busy preparing her store,
"Good morrow now Johnny," as she opened the door.

Ned Coffey the postman, I would see out the road,
To post office he'd pedal, from his humble abode,
The letters to sort, and store in his bag,
Then away on his bike, with the puff of a fag.

The grinding of gravel 'neath steel banded wheels,
Moss Leary, his ass and well painted creels,
A fill of dry turf he'd bring home from the bog,
To warm his mother, himself and the dog.

The creamery now open and ready to go,
Horse carts with milk tanks all lined in a row,
The farmers discussing the weather and hay,
Tom Lynch in his white coat would bid them "good day."

The laughter of children at play 'round the school,
Eleven o'clock being the time as a rule,
When the master would send them outside for a break,
While he and Miss Summers, the fresh air to take.

The Village

The Angelus bell at noon it would toll,
Bringing reverend bow to each village soul,
The ploughman would call his brace to a stand,
And whisper a prayer, with cap in his hand.

Then down to the stream by the church I would stray,
And gaze at Pat Sullivan whiling the day,
Spinning and casting a fly hook about,
Hoping to bag that elusive brown trout.

'Round the old bridge and up the steep hill,
The waterwheel merrily turning its mill.
Its owner Jack Maher chanting away,
Happily toiling for all of the day.

On down from the forge, a-walking his mare,
I'd meet Bateen Doody with devil a care.
He'd share all the news from auld Jackeen Gow's,
Before heading for home, to milk his few cows.

Standing, I watch Bateen fade in the past,
Along with this hamlet and wonderful cast,
Sadly, reality soon will take o'er,
My village of dreams will be never- no-more.

THE MISSION

By Anne McCarthy

'This is flight Commander Blackeye to all commandos. Prepare for take-off.'

"Aye, aye Captain," the team replied together.

Commander Blackeye smiled. His unit was the best in the regiment. They were well trained pilots, ready to carry out manoeuvres on command. His lieutenants were disciplined and excellent at following procedure, alert and reactive in enemy territory.

'Let's fly over the township first to check for target bases,' he ordered.

Once they flew high into the sky, they were above the sound barrier and could survey the landscape unnoticed. The team enjoyed this part of the mission. There was always friendly competition amongst them to see who could locate touchdown units first. Black Feather was normally the sharpest in the team. However since the new Chick joined the crew, he was lagging behind. Blackeye rued the day that females were given freedom to enlist. Those lassies were better employed at base, he thought. He knew, however, that he had better keep his beak shut or he would be reprimanded by the Higher Authority.

"Captain, this is Cawker 101. I have positive identification of target at lines 20-14. Can you confirm with me?"

'Affirmative Cawker. Check for enemy on site,' he replied.

"No one in sight. Oh hang on! We have one enemy Sir. He's got something in his hand."

'Is it a gun Cawker?' Blackeye demanded.

"Actually, it looks like bread Sir, sliced bread. I'll check it out Sir."

'Be careful Cawker.'

Cawker swooped close to the target base and identified a young boy as a friendly enemy. His team followed him once positive identification was confirmed.

They landed close to the enemy line and watched as the boy flung broken bits of bread onto the ground. They had experienced the boy on previous missions and he had proven to be trustworthy. The enemy was known to have laced bread with poison resulting in untimely casualties in their regiment in the past.

Black Feather was the most daring of the team. He took risks because he liked to show off in front of the team. Up until now he had been lucky. He landed close to where the young boy was standing. The boy smiled with a glassy glaze in his eye.

Black Feather extended his wings wide in greeting. Quickly he snapped up a piece of white bread with his beak and gobbled it. It was delicious. It was so much tastier than the greasy leftovers outside the chipper on a Sunday morning. His team mates perched excitedly on the fence leaving a trail of large white droppings on the brown timber. Once the all-clear was given, they swooped down and feasted.

Suddenly a little girl ran from the house, shouting at the boy. The team quickly retreated back up to the top of the fence.
"Shoo, shoo!" she shouted at them waving her arms. "Go away."
"Jackie," she reprimanded the little boy. "Mammy says you're not to feed the crows. They do kaka all over the fence and Mr Higgins, next door, gets really mad. Put it into the bin here instead."
'But Mammy gets cross if I don't eat my crusts,' Jackie whined.
"Look you can hide them under the carrot peel in the brown bin. She'll never know. Quick hurry, I think I can hear Mr Higgins's car pull into the driveway."
A car door slammed in the distance. She ran over towards the crows whispering ferociously "Shoo, shoo!"
'All units return to base immediately,' Captain Blackeye commanded.

Flying high over the township, the team practised synchronised gliding. The Aviation Olympics were coming up shortly and they were determined to beat the swallows and be the best in the air. It would be good for the regiment and crows in general to have an Olympic win. Crows really didn't have a great name on the planet.

In the distance a small wood of ageing pine trees came into view. Captain Blackeye heaved a sigh of relief that his whole team had returned to base unscathed. Tomorrow would be another day.

GIVING UP
By Cáit Curtain

Embers glow in a cobbled hearth:
Shadows flicker on white washed walls;
Moonlight seeps through slatted blinds;
Eerie quiet as darkness falls.

Stiffly she rises from her rocking chair,
Her red-gold hair now tinged with grey.
Slowly she climbs the well worn stairs
Her passage lit by the pale moon's rays.

She pauses at a bedroom door,
Lifts the latch and peeps inside.
The night light shows a tousled head,
The wheelchair by the low bedside

Pictures of his football heroes —
Rugby, golf and hurling too;
His school companions grouped together
His parents and their dog called *Blue*.

Giving Up

Only a short while ago he'd sported
Without worry or a care;
The light glinting on the wheelchair
Meant a halt to work and play.

Though today the clouds seemed darker,
He never moaned about ill luck;
Just squared his youthful shoulders,
Affirmed, I'm not giving up.

Gently the door's back on the latch,
The moon lights up the way.
She returns to the warm hearth
To await a brand new day.

Her heart is filled with a mother's pride
At his courage, faith and pluck.
She swears upon her Rosary beads
She is never giving up.

OCTOBER NIGHT

By Marian Pender

'Wait' he said, 'She hasn't got her hat on!' Brendan's instruction seemed to accuse the lighting with which the cameraman tinkered.

I was attired in one of Great Aunt Minnie's classics; vintage black taffeta detailed with *embroidre anglaise*. It's bodice, a simple, sleeveless crossover, with deep V's both front and back would have preferred a cleavage more substantial than mine. But the stiff, shiny silk whispered and whooshed as I swung my hips, while a full circle skirt swirled and fell in elegant folds from my tiny waist and made up for it. From the same old American trunk, nestled in cobwebs at the far recess of the attic, came her shoes; dark and lustrous black soft kid peep-toes. Feeling good, I watched as they shimmered in the glow of the October gibbous moon, and the occasional wobble due to their height was steadied by my brother, and escort for the night, with a stiff hand in my back.

The photographer's flash surprised the frock's shocking pink lining; it flared and flickered through the minutely-stitched, tear-shaped black holes in the magnesium light as a whispered *wow* from behind the camera reached our ears. 'Wait', said my twin, once again addressing the light and handing me the fur stole.

I pretended not to notice the forgotten fragrance of Anais Anais mixed with mothballs that rose on the still night air. I stroked the stole's softness as I draped the joined pelts over my shoulders, visualising Great Aunt Minnie on a night out; one pair of foxes, tailed together at the back, their faces nestling the nape of her neck; while the second pair with their rumps beneath the paws, toes and curled nails of the first, descended glassy-eyed down her bosom, until their faces, ears and snouts met and clasped each other with braided hooks.

October Night

Then, an encouraging cheer broke from the darkness, accompanied by a veritable fireworks of artificial lighting in response to Brendan's *ready*. My ensemble, now complete with tall black pointed hat and plastic orange bucket, was recorded for posterity and enabled my brother and I to take off into the witching night, as only nine year olds can.

THE VILLAGE OF TALBOT'S INCH

By James Flynn

A cottage is the place for me, somewhere I always want to be,
And when its name is Talbot's Inch it has warmth in history.
Lady Desart built this place with character and style,
<u>For working folk on her estate engaged at honest toil</u>.

An age when darkness dimmed the souls of folk throughout the land,
When parents prayed and children cried, 'twas hard to understand.
The village folk were treated right considering those days,
<u>In spite of dark imaginings, it was a lucky place.</u>

The scent of woodbine lures the bee as sun sets in the west,
The village is a haven now, it's the time I love the best.
It's haunted by the noble ghosts of bygone chequered years,
<u>By happiness and sadness too, and a mother's gentle tears.</u>

I love these walls, these hallowed walls, full of such wondrous tales
Of working folk and gentle things and life's unyielding gales.
And it is good to look outside and view the village green,
<u>Protective of the old world charm that captivates the scene.</u>

The Village of Talbot's Inch

The kings of handball came here too well worthy of the name,
With lightning speed and awesome skill, they played this crafty game.
Sportsmen true of great renown, they filled us with delight;
<u>The gentle folk of Talbot's Inch remember them each night.</u>

And even when I'm far away I long for its fond embrace,
And to the station I will go to find this lovely place.
This refuge from a wretched world, that place that I call home;
<u>I have no need for all this greed, no longer will I roam.</u>

So call me selfish, call me vain but I don't even care,
I'll spend my days in this dear place so beautiful and rare.
With working folk and gentle things, the things of long ago,
<u>At Talbot's Inch you'll find all this, where ever you may go.</u>

I've seen the Kingdom's beauty and its heavenly desires,
And places where our artists and poets are inspired.
But Talbot's Inch is different; it's a dream within a dream;
And, at the evening of my life, confers me with esteem.

THE SUMMONS
By Bridie Callanan

As soon as I arrived I could sense something was out of place, even more intently now than the nagging feeling that haunted me ever since I had received Mam's letter. Mam & Dad resisted change as stubbornly as the craggy cliffs and out crops of the black valley to the forces of nature. Phones, computers & TV. Time wasters, Dad would say, and Mam's silence would signify agreement.

Her letter was Spartan in content as usual, but none the less her strange request asking to see me had me sensing something was out of place. "Nothing to worry about, but come even for a few days if you get a chance," she had written. This uneasy feeling had forced me on to a plane and hurried me half way across the world. My anxiety level was certainly none the better having sat for up to twenty four hours in a hollowed out aluminium can at thirty five thousand feet.

The house had changed little, pristine whitewash against strong grey hills and a watery sky. Fire engine red windows and doors —old or new age! The thatch was gone; replaced with slate, but I knew this from Mary, the youngest of us, who emailed me from Boston. She chose to join Patrick, our youngest and only brother. We kept in touch through e-mail and Skype for the past eight years. We were like chalk and cheese, go with the flow was her motto; life is too short and fragile.

She went home every few years and kept me in touch with the goings on.

What in heavens' name were all the cars parked along the front stone wall? The boreen had black bitumen now and fluorescent white lines in the centre even though it was only the width of a car, and a small one at that. On numerous occasions I had to pull in to a gap to facilitate the passing of oncoming cars. Only a few of the drivers reciprocated my courtesy.

I left my bags in the boot, keeping my hands free for the welcoming, not that I expected a full body hugging embrace. Mam and Dad were never ones for ostentatious displays of emotions, something I would have loved, but didn't have the courage.

There was music and laughter coming towards me on the mist of the evening as I approached the house – Was I too late? Was it a wake? Surely there would be a more sombre mood on such an occasion. Mam and Dad never drank and if one was gone surely the other would not allow it, unless the two were gone. Then again how could she have foreseen their deaths? A suicide pact! Nonsense! What about the fires of hell, Mam! Calm down, get yourself together; the moment of truth is at hand.

As I lifted the latch I braced myself. The door swung open. I blinked, my jaw dropped, my mind numbed. Had I stepped into another dimension? I gave a nervous glance back as I closed the door to the familiar stony hills.

The Summons

The house was full, some I recognised as old neighbours, the rest were strangers. Mary and Patrick were sitting with their backs to me on white leather covered chrome stools at a kitchen that mirrored the chrome, with its white high gloss drawers without handles, and polished granite top. Shanghai marble, it was later explained to me — harder and cheaper than Connemara marble. Imagine that, Dad said.

Mam was sitting with Aunty Kathleen on a white leather lounge wearing a red dress that highlighted her raven hair and soft complexion. She looked ten years younger than my memory of her, and that was ten years ago. Dad was watching an Irish Folk Band on a plasma TV that would have sufficed as a partition in the old kitchen. The back wall of the house was gone. The kitchen opened out to the valley and the black river that flowed past our house to the Killarney Lakes. The view was enclosed by sliding glass walls on a marble floor, the roof extended upwards in an arch — a scene out of Vogue.

The tiger had been through the valley for Dad and Mam in the shape of a wealthy foreign speculator who paid four million euro for fifty acres of hill side only sheep and goats could navigate. Plans for a five star hotel were drawn and approved. Dad had use of the land until the construction started. That was eight years ago. The tiger is long gone back to Asia or China.

Unsure of their good fortune and fearful the speculator would return to take their money back they kept quiet and left it sitting in the Bank. By now the interest alone was worth a fortune. Finally they had come to terms with their luck and our modern world.

The Summons

Sitting opposite the two of them in First Class on our way from Boston to Sydney, Mam with her I Phone on flight mode and Dad reading a book on his Kindle, I realised some truths - that the opulence of First-Class sure enhances the experiences of flying, and fear is lost in the luxury of the surroundings and the attentiveness of the hostesses.

I'll finish with two quotations they'd do well to heed:-

'Money is like love; it kills slowly and painfully the one who withholds it, and enlivens the other who turns it on his fellow man.' Khalil Gibran

'When I had money, money, O!
I knew no joy till I went poor;
For many a false man as a friend
Came knocking all day at my door'. William Davies

MY YOUNGEST

By Lorraine Carey

Your earth-brown eyes,
DNA from your father
like Galaxy chocolate,
Ebony lashed,
that would stir envy
in pubescent girls.

Those apple cheeks —
Perfect little spheres
that have felt my million kisses —
Tinged scarlet tonight,
from Etna-erupted gums.

Your moist little chin,
I try to keep dribble free.
Immaculate skin,
blushing new,
softer than a velvety peach
encloses you from toe to head.

My Youngest

Bath time complete,
you wriggle on my lap.
Ensconced in a breeze wrapped towel
your baby hands try to catch dancing dust,
somersaulting, caught in sunrays
poking through Venetian blinds.

Later, you navigate through your
drowsy consciousness.
A straight path to sleep.
Under a sky punctuated with stars
punched into the sooty ceiling
above ornate earth.

In the glow of soft lamplight,
I murmur goodnight
to those saucer eyes,
heavily lidded,

falling under…

those lustrous lashes joining
for the night.

My Favourite Place

By Frank Kevins

It was a mid-July day when I first laid eyes on the venue which would become my favourite place. I was eleven years old. The previous day I had fallen off a donkey's back when it suddenly shied from a paper bag lying in the middle of the road. My elbow took the weight of my body when I hit the ground.

My older sister was given the task of taking me to see the doctor. I was relieved when the doctor examined my arm, and diagnosed that I had only chipped my elbow. He said it would heal itself without needing a plaster cast. He gave me a sling to wear for a few days.

After we left the doctor's surgery, my sister sprang a surprise by saying we were going to the Killarney Races that afternoon. I felt a sense of adventure, and anticipation as we walked the short distance to the course. It would be my first visit to a racecourse, and I did not know what to expect.

When we reached the entrance to the track, a man in a purple suit was calling out "Roll up, roll up, I have a horse." and added "For half a crown I will tell you the name of one that is catching pigeons at home." Further along a huddle of people were trying to solve the mystery of the three card trick. I was left wondering if anyone would solve that conundrum.

The clinking and clonking of the turnstiles as we passed through them, felt like we had entered a magical world, where reality was suspended. As we walked into the racecourse, the most colourful scene was laid out in front of us. With a majestic backdrop of mountains, lakes, and a castle, it looked like a page from a fairy-tale. The unspoiled wildness of the scenery contrasted with the manmade and manicured track, with its white running rail, grandstand, bar, and restaurant. The smell of new mown grass, perfume, fresh flowers, and roasting meat were drifting and mingling together to create a unique festival atmosphere. We sat on the grass, soaking up the sunshine, and admiring the fashion on display.

The outfits that the ladies wore showed great imagination, and original-ity, especially the hats. Broad brimmed tilted to the side, were a favourite, with a variety of trimming which included, curled feathers, ribbons and bows, quirky quills, orange lilies, black roses, and were often finished with netting. A 'best dressed lady' contest took place later in the day, and a prize awarded to the winner.

The bookmakers, whose names included Lucky Joe, Bold Barney, and Dixie O'Dea added to the occasion with their coloured umbrellas, and were calling out the odds to entice the crowd to have a flutter. A tic-tac man wearing white gloves was busy letting the bookies know of changes in the betting odds with his unique hand signals.

The time of the first race was approaching, so we made our way to the parade ring to see the horses close up. Seeing the horses walk around, it was clear that they all had different personalities. Some walked with a swagger, some kept their heads down, and others made eye contact with the spectators. Being near the horses had a calming effect on the crowd, and it was noticeable how people were talking softly, as they watched the horses being led by their stable staff.

The jockeys entered the parade ring, and each made their way to the trainers and owners of their mounts, to discuss tactics. Within a few minutes the announcement "Jockeys please mount" was heard. Then each rider located his horse, and was eased into the saddle. As the horses came out onto the course they were eager to get into their galloping stride, and show us how well they moved on the way to the start. The sound of them snorting, and blowing from their airways, mixed with the noise their hooves made on the turf was infectious.

The horses were milling around at start for a few minutes, before we heard the course commentator say "They're under starters orders" followed shortly by "They're off." The noise, passion and excitement rose as the horses came past the stands for the first time. The crowd strained to see the colours of the horses they had backed, and shouted encouragement to the jockeys. The splash of vibrant colours traveling at speed caused them to fuse into a blur.

I was standing with my sister near the rail, so I could get a close-up of the action. The horses went out of our sight for about a minute, and when they came back into view, they were turning into the straight. At first I could only see the jockey's caps on the horizon. They appeared like multi - coloured beach balls bobbing on a sea of green. When they came fully into view, they were galloping at full speed, with whips rising and falling on the horses, and the riders were jostling for position to make their final effort.

The commentator's voice was at fever pitch, as the runners came inside the final furlong. I felt the ground shake like a mini earthquake as the runners flashed past. The crowd were screaming, and jumping up to catch a better view of the finish. Two horses were stride for stride, ahead of the field as they raced up to the line inseparable. "Photo finish" shouts the commentator.

From that moment on I was hooked. The mixture of escapism, adrenaline, colour, excitement, passion, and witnessing the partnership of humans and the noblest of animals, in a glorious setting, is nature at its finest.

PETAL WISHES

By Judith Carmody

My heart is warm and full of love
Like a flower opens, blossoms and buds.

With each soft pink and yellow petal
I wish to share its joy about.

My first petal wish is to set you free,
To break away from all that fear.

My second petal wish is to give you love,
That makes your heart soar like a dove.

My third petal wish is to give you wisdom,
To give you strength to reach god's kingdom.

My fourth petal wish is to give you peace,
You'll only find it when you're heart's at ease.

My fifth petal wish is to give you clarity,
So that your time is full of charity.

Petal Wishes

My sixth petal wish is to give you truth,
Without it, you're lost on a darkened route.

My final petal wish is to give you, You,
To love, cherish and protect in all you do.

There is only one of you on this earth,
Chosen by god in his great concept.

Go only in the light that shines bright
Each morn greet the sun, smile and feel its light.

They Lived "The Happy Ever After Life" Or So It Seemed.

Elsie McDonald

Standing tall in his designer shoes and hand finished suit, he held a manly pose. One hand in pocket and a gentle lilt to the right cast a subtle pointer towards the brand new jaguar sports car delivered just this morning.

The pale, silver-blue, bodywork complemented the grey shades of marble steps that wound their way upwards to the imposing entrance of the spacious manor. Solid glass doors, thick and boldly engraved, arched with fragrant garlands of pale pink roses framed the point of welcome.

She appeared, like a bride in her wedding gown, elegant, graceful, exquisitely formed. Without descending, she cast her beautiful green eyes over the scene below, and then she was gone.

The engine roared as he played with his new toy, foot to the floor, throwing himself from side to side as he sped through the twists and turns of the private estate until, with a screech of brakes, he narrowly missed the heavy metal gates of the walled garden.

That's where it all began, just beyond the magnolia tree. It was a hot sunny day, they sat down to a picnic of pork pie, cheese sandwiches and fruit cake, washed down with homemade lemonade. The birds sang in the trees and he knew that he would hold that moment for ever.

Just a week earlier, below stairs a young girl rubbed the sleep from her eyes; it was only five a.m. She dressed quickly and pushed on with her many chores. The work was hard, not that she was afraid of hard work, but there was little reward.

The buzzer sounded, and, as a dog runs at the master's whistle, she responded instantly, carrying a tray dressed with the crisp clean napkin, freshly washed, starched and ironed. She made her way up the stairs savouring the aroma rising from the plate of grilled bacon, eggs and mushrooms. By now it was seven thirty, and as yet not a morsel had passed her lips.

Outside, the sit-on mower rumbled along the lawns, her heart missed a beat as her thoughts turned to the young man at the helm. The highlights of her day were the shared ten o'clock and lunch breaks. She envied his freedom to leave at the end of the day. He would park his bicycle under the drying canopy, if the washing was finished in time, she could be pegging out as he collects it.

It didn't go unnoticed. A few weeks later the garden fell silent, no cutting, digging or mowing and no gardener. Nothing was said, and everything went on as usual.

The rolls had been sent for, a rare occurrence, which usually indicated some business had to be attended to. Helping the elderly man into his seat, she couldn't help but notice a change in him, he looked frail, his hands were shaking and he seemed ill at ease.

On his return, some hours later, without taking refreshment, he took to his bed and never raised his head from it again. Seventy odd years didn't yield many friends or acquaintances, a meagre number stood at the graveside. The funeral over she wondered what would become of her now. She returned to her room seeking solace in the familiar, and fixed her gaze on the old buzzer. She was startled out of her thoughts by a knock at the door. She tentatively moved up stairs pondering the wisdom of opening the door. Through the glass she discerned the familiar form of the gardener; he held her so tight she ran out of breath. Absence had made the heart grow fonder and he had a burning question that needed an answer. Would she marry him? Of course she would.

They Lived "The Happy Ever After Life" Or So It Seemed

Before making any such plans, there was the business of the will to be read the next day. Well suited men arrived summoning her to the drawing room. They asked her to sit. Fearing the worst, she obliged; she had never taken such a liberty before. Aghast she listened to the words "all my worldly goods I leave to my granddaughter".

"Granddaughter "she repeated and shook herself in disbelief, it was all hers, everything.

The Happy ever after life was about to become a reality, she couldn't wait to tell the gardener. The hours slowly ticked away until the sound of his bicycle grated over the small stones outside. She ran out to greet him and he stopped her in her tracks. His handsome face was pale and troubled. He too had an appointment that day, the solicitor delivered the blow.

"In fulfilment of my promise to your mother, I leave you, my illegitimate grandson, £200,000 and the Jaguar car she said you had always dreamed of.

DECEASED IN DECEMBER

By Lorraine Carey

I walked in on you
trying to thread a needle, without your glasses.

Refusing help, you persevered, dodging the eye
like a blindfolded gannet
spearing waves, not fish.

A nervous dart evading a bulls-eye,
you relented and passed me old thread.

Vampire thread that had not seen sunlight for a sewing box
eternity stood huddled in sparse spools.
These spools of jaded rainbows,
in the old biscuit tin since Grandmother died.

Her death brought gossamer-like shroud that enveloped you.
Your jeans, striving to stay up and around your waist,
only just – despite the absence of a button.
They symbolised the abyss, a tearful mist.

And you, my Grandfather,
just wanted Mary.

HOPE

By Sharon Fitzpatrick

It was in the middle of the night, pitch black outside. I was in my luxurious King Size bed, having the most wonderful sleep. All of a sudden I woke to the sound of a loud phone ringing. Even though I was in a deep sleep, I instinctively rushed out of bed.

My heart, beating at treble speed, it felt like it was trying to get out of my chest. I got up in such a hurry, I was shaking; my little legs were wobbling uncontrollably. Disorientated and not knowing what was happening, I picked up the phone and all I heard was weird breathing, not a word from the caller on the other end.

I stomped back to my bed and lay wide awake looking at the ceiling. How dare a crank caller ring just to get his kicks? I wanted to see the creep hang by his testicles. Feeling really disgruntled and trying my best to relax back to dreamland, the stupid phone rang again. I tried to ignore it, but couldn't. Slowly I got to my feet and walked to the phone, this time realising it was Sheila's number on the caller I.D. display. Realisation suddenly dawned on me. Putting my ear to the phone, I listened carefully. I could hear the hoarse breathing again.

My heart speeded up again. I dropped the phone, got into my slippers, grabbed my keys and ran next door. Her bedroom light was on, but the door was locked. Thankfully I had a spare key she had given me, in case she locked herself out like last month. My hands were shaking so much; I couldn't even put the key in the lock. Frustrated, I stood there talking to myself, telling myself to calm down and take deep breaths. Composed, I finally get the key in. In my haste, I left it in the lock and the door open and ran up those stairs like an Olympian.

Hope

I hurried to her room. There lovely old Sheila was, collapsed on the floor next to the phone. I called 999. Despite the fact I was in a terrible state the lady I spoke to was fantastic. She somehow managed to calm me down and I was able to follow her instructions. She talked me through what I had to do until the ambulance came.

Eventually after what felt like hours, I heard the all familiar sound of the sirens. When the paramedics came and took over, I just sat on the floor, hugging my knees and cried like a big babbling baby.

I followed them down stairs and sat in the ambulance with her, watching her unconscious body strapped up. I sat and prayed hard all the way to the hospital. They hurried her away to the doctors' area, while I was made to wait in a room. Pacing up and down, I must have lost a stone in weight. The nurse came in, with a smile on her face that said enough. She told me what room she was in. I peeped my head in the door and she looked up at me between tubes and the drip. Her eyes lit up when she saw me. I was so relieved to see that lovely face alive again.

REMEMBERING JULIA

By Helen Blanchfield

As I walk along the leaf-fringed roads
In the Currow once dear to you,
I think of you sweet Julia Barry
When you walked these roadways too.
In my mind's eye I see you
In Dicksgrove and Parkmore,
Soaking in those views through your soft eyes
Before you left your native shore.

Twas as awake when you first left
Bound for Americae,
Where exiles ne'er saw home again
A happy visit home you paid.
Michael Barry embraced his daughter
Leaving Currow once again
April fourteenth 1912
At one thirty in the P.M.

To board a floating palace
Upstairs they danced all night till dawn.
Did you imagine their lavish merriment
Or did Johann Strauss come flittering down?
Below the bows with comrades dear
Perhaps you were as content,
Where thoughts of home and memories shared
Precious moments were well spent.

Remembering Julia

Was it the crash, the sirens blare,
Or the frantic cries that woke you
To run that maze of passageways
To the upper deck open to so few?
For the sea was calm and the sky was bright
When that maiden voyage hit panic.
Did you get to taste its cold crisp air,
Or remain in Belly of Titanic?

When I think of the crowds weeping,
Violins playing and families sorrow,
Did you take solace in a children's prayer
That you learned in school in Currow?
For as your parish must have mourned you then
Now one hundred years have passed,
We think of you with fondness Julia,
We'll make your memory last.

ACCIDENT ?

By Fiona Roche

Coiling, Winding, Failing, Mating
A daughter born
Dark yet fair.

It is she who will care
For those who
Called her an accident.

Unwanted, yet wanted,
A journey taken.
Here but not,
A tiptoe walker.
Accidental she.

Imagine life without
This accident!
There are — no accidents.

THE WAKE

By Madeline O' Connor

In rural Ireland certain traditions were observed round various occasions, one of these was the wake. On the passing of a person the first thing to be done was to alert the parish clergy and the sacristan who rang the church bell to spread the news that a death had occurred in the parish. Three rings were made for a man and two for a woman.

After that the news spread by word of mouth. The creamery in the morning was a good place to hear the news of the parish. There was usually a woman in the locality who took on the job of laying out the deceased in a long brown garment known as a habit which had a cross embossed on the front. They also came in blue for women who were enrolled in a devotion called Children of Mary.

In the house all mirrors were covered and the clock was turned face down. Time stood still. At the wake women were offered port wine and biscuits; sometimes snuff was passed around as well, while the men indulged in a glass of whiskey or porter. In earlier years clay pipes were smoked.

The digging of the grave.

If the death occurred at the weekend a sod would have to be turned on the grave on Sunday as it was considered bad luck to open a grave on Monday. The grave was dug by neighbours of the deceased and a bottle of whiskey was supplied to them to help them with the job. The clergy wore white sashes of linen at the funeral. The hearse was mostly horse drawn. Food at the wake consisted of tea and barm brack and jam.

The deceased clothes were given to a close friend of the family who was obliged to wear them for three consecutive Sundays to Mass. The question might be asked after a funeral by neighbours — I wonder who will get the clothes? It was considered a privilege to be the one chosen by a family.

The bereaved family observed a period of mourning, usually a year. They abstained from all social activities like dancing etc. Widows wore black and often continued to do so for the rest of their lives. They might be referred as the widow woman after that and received a lot of compassion and help from neighbours. Men wore a diamond shaped crape on their sleeves for a year after the death. These were the customs then, long before funeral homes were heard of.

MOUNT EAGLE

By James Flynn

Remote from all the traffic and the din,
Mount Eagle inclines happiness within,
Between Castleisland and homely Brosna town,
As rare a spot as ever could be found.

Its lovely woods that whisper sheltered peace,
And nature's beauty primed for its release;
The harmony of bird song at the dawn,
Wild game and goats that wander on Sliabh Bán.

The buttercups and roses that delight:
The playful swallow teasing in its flight;
Blackwater River babbles its refrain
Of life and death, of happiness and pain.

'Twas down its mountain road I stepped with Dad
When I was ten years old and just a lad.
When I was fifty he was eighty four,
Still roaming woodland tracks, but now no more.

Perhaps on earth a paradise we found
Where beauty sings, and happy thoughts abound.
Perhaps in death our spirits will entwine
On dear Mount Eagle's woods and steep incline.

A JOURNEY
By
Anne Coffey

Phil and I decided we would go on a visit to Rome. We organized ourselves, along with thirty other people from Cork city to journey with us. We arrived at Cork Airport, excited as we all boarded the plane together. We were eagerly looking forward to our journey. We arrived in Rome three and a half hours later with a great round of applause from all the passengers.

We met our courier who took us to our hotel, a kilometre away. We were given our room numbers and details of our activities for the week. After our delicious breakfast, we had Mass and then journeyed to lots of different sights.

Everyone threw in some coins to Trevi fountain, took some pictures in St. Peter's square and saw the window where the Pope gives his blessing to the people. The place oozed richness. The Sistine chapel where we had to cover our heads, was amazing.

Every night passengers and the bishop sang a song. Very enjoyable evenings. I bought a beautiful art picture of the Coliseum, from an artist on the street for ten euro. I had it framed when I came home. It looks beautiful on my sitting room wall and every one admires it when they come to visit.

A wonderful reminder for me of my fabulous memorable journey to Rome.

ANGEL OF MINE

By Judith Carmody

A soft white feather floats above me
Belonging to my angel I cannot see.
A warm feeling snuggles around me,
My angel near and protecting me.

This tiny feather pauses on me.
I caress its welcome vision to me.
A lovely sign from heaven above,
No more panic; nor even fear.

I am sworn to secrecy
Only to tell to those who understand
I must be quiet, and wonder in awe
Of the brightest light that's all around.

The sweet aura of being a chosen one —
Who need not be lost or lonely anymore.
Even though I cannot see,
I know you're there, guiding me.

I blossom in this radiance of true love
And cherish it as a pure white dove.
Darkness is banished for ever more,
I chose to love and live to adore.

He Looked Into the Blazing Fire
By Ann Kiely

He looked into the blazing fire, speechless at what he saw. We were visiting my relations in the neighbouring parish in the late fifties. I will always remember my Uncle aghast at the flames as they soared up the chimney. Although it is many moons ago, I remember as if it was now, we immediately had to draw buckets of water to put out the fire. Thank God the chimney did not catch fire.

They had a wide hearth in the kitchen where a big pot was put on the fire for boiling water, cooking meals and baking bread. There was a hook to move the utensils around the hanging rack. Each member of the family got their chance of turning the wheel to blow the bellows to give wind to the fire, so the pot would boil quicker. Nora would race through the kitchen so she would not have to sit and turn the wheel. Such drudgery did not fit in her plans! Wild as a March hare's hopping party, her mind was always somewhere else; the days were not long enough for her.

Out in the fields playing hide-and-go-seek with the brothers and sisters, the countryside was their play-ground. School holidays were not long enough for them at all, but the modern era was stealing up on them. A Stanley range would be fitted in the kitchen. Electricity poles were sprouting along the road and eventually marched single-file up the hill. Everything from now on would be at a flick of a switch; no more hard work, or so they thought. If Nora did not watch it she would become even more lazy, as everything in those days was very labour intensive, earning your bread by the sweat of your brow. But time moves on and it is great to witness many changes over the years.

He Looked Into the Blazing Fire

Nora was up early to get the fire started, as it took some time to heat the old black kettle. There was no such thing as going the chipper for take-away food; the people of that generation did not put on any weight. They never heard of diets, and exercises were what you got as homework from school. They developed strong bones as they had to walk everywhere. The lucky ones might have access to a bike to cycle to school, church or shop. The youngsters were always out in the fresh air and slept all night; no sleeping pills then, and you did not go to the Doctor's unless you really were ill.

Getting back to the blazing fire in the hearth in the long ago — the black no 8 range came to Nora's home. Her father got a man to block off the fire place. She got a bit of a shock when she came home from school to see a block wall where the fire-place used to be. She felt a sense of loss; it was the end of an era. Open fires draws neighbours together in the long winter nights; conversation flows easily. There was a gap to be filled in the hearth. A door was fitted and one of the brothers decided to put bags of coal in there, it would save them going out in the dark on a cold winter's night. The range was connected up with a pipe to take the smoke into the hearth and up the chimney, but of course they forgot about sparks from the coal and timber from the range. Boy did it blaze! All four bags of coal made a beautiful fire! We opened the door and poured on plenty of water to quench the fire. They were very innocent in those days but a lesson was learned to stay with us for the rest of our lives — not to mess with fires.

WATER

By Jimmy Cullinane

You can draw it from the river,
You may drink it from the well,
You will find it blessed in the church
To consign Old Nick to hell.

You will need it every morning
To make that pot of tae.
You'll find it's great to kill the thirst
As you go about your day.

You can drill a bore hole for it,
Then install an electric pump.
Drawing water is laborious,
It can give the body a hump.

We need it to wash the crockery
To make it bright and clean;
Also to wash the window panes
The daylight to be seen.

We need it to shower our bodies to keep us clean and fresh.
There is a cure in salt and water; it restores battered skin and flesh.

You will find it in the gutters
As soon as it starts to rain,
You will see it on the footpaths
And running down the window pane.

You will see it flowing the river
The colour of yellow mud;
It must have rained all night long
There is a real big flood.

Water

Water is needed every day at Abattoir and slaughter.
No matter how high a bird will fly, it must still come down for water.

We visit public toilets each and every day;
We waste a lot of water when we know we need not pay.

Water is scarce in many places, much more than we think.
You may take the horse to water but you cannot make him drink.

Bottling water is big business,
It is stocked on many shelves.
There is no need to buy it —
Just a little planning for ourselves.

And now to end my *Uisce* poem,
The old saying does not lie —
You will never miss the water
Until the well runs dry.

BROWN FLESK AT NIGHT
By Helen Blanchfield

Glistening waters
That float on by.
How mystical thou art,
How still am I?

My awe at thy beauty
Just water, just stone
And whimsical thoughts
As I stand here alone.

Oh mighty three arches
What ghosts have you seen?
Of hopes and of dreamers
From this century and then.

Go carve out your beauty
Where pathways are shorn
And life undetermined
Where water may flow.

The moonlight your mother
To highlight your grace.
Tears of a mother
Knowing forever your face.

So bubble and bustle
And busy along;
Your pace is your heartbeat
Your gushing, your song

THE PARTY

By Madeline O' Connor

Rising early as usual Judith skipped downstairs. The kettle on, she lifted the blind and glanced out the window. It promised to be a glorious day, the day Peter and she would celebrate their fortieth wedding anniversary. They would host a great party later that evening for family and friends. Peter was delighted when some high ranking officers from the police force had accepted the invitation. He had joined the force himself some ten years previously. The post of superintendent was to become vacant in October when the present officer retired. He wanted to make a good impression which might help his career prospects later.

Four decades together, Judith and Peter had a good marriage. Of course there were some rocky times especially when Peter had to work unsociable hours or travel away from home. Judith loved to entertain their friends and she still looked pretty good for her age. Their son and heir Cyril had recently joined the force and was stationed in the city. He was getting time off to be with his parents on their happy occasion. He was bringing his girlfriend with him. It would be the first time they had met her, but had got the message she was someone special. Judith was already anxious about meeting her. Nobody was ever going to be good enough for her much loved son.

The Party

The aroma of bacon wafting up the stairs encouraged Peter to get out of bed sooner than he had planned. After breakfast Judith had a long list of chores that would keep him busy until lunchtime.

"Lots to do," she said. "I want it all to be perfect before everybody arrives." Making sure the garden was tidy, tables and chairs set up in the marquee and the bar stocked, were among the orders doled out. The marquee was already set up in the garden next to the swimming pool in case anybody needed to take a dip. The musicians arrived during the afternoon to set up their equipment. By six o'clock the caterers had arrived with a huge variety of food.

Peter and Judith checked everything was right before changing into their evening wear. Peter in his smart suit and Judith in her full length black designer number with sequined jacket. The party was already in full swing by the time Cyril arrived with a very attractive, but somewhat older woman on his arm. "Mum, Dad, I'd like to introduce you to my fiancée, Lucy. We got engaged last night but I wanted to tell you in person." Beaming away, totally unaware of his parents shocked reaction he added, "I know you are going to love her as much as I do."

"I'm so very pleased to meet you at last. I've heard so much about you," Lucy gushed as she pecked Judith on the cheek. She turned to Peter who didn't wait to greet her but rather rudely turned away and disappeared into the marquee. Cyril apologised profusely for his father's behaviour, blaming the stress of the occasion for his actions. Privately though he thought it was inexcusable. Judith mingled among the guests pretending everything was fine. But she couldn't figure out why her husband had reacted like he did. He also kept avoiding her — and this was their party. Cyril had a puzzled look on his face, while Lucy seemed to be thoroughly enjoying herself.

As Judith was seeing off the first guests to leave at midnight, she spotted Peter roughly grabbing Lucy by the arm at the entrance to the marquee. "You have got to break it off with Cyril," she heard him snap at her. "Nobody must ever know what happened," he added. "Peter dear, nobody dumps me and gets away with it," Lucy answered with a grin.

LOYALTY AND GRACE

In Memory Of Joseph Mary Plunkett

By Helen Blanchfield

Five dragons crush the souls within that deathly dank and cold forbidden place
Where man may ne'er see home again, his weakened limbs endeavour for to pace.
Yet deep within that dragon burns a love, and a loyalty so strong to turn the tide.
Proficient plans nurtured for so long and greatly proud to stand at Pearse's side.

A candle flickers in the chapel pane and guides a sovereign ring to slender hand.
Just two soldiers hear their soft refrain, a futile future sealed by this wedding band.
And did the tears mist up your rounded glass or fall upon your blooded neckerchief?
In hapless haste they counted down, before you went to die for your belief.

Sweet Grace my love, my heart's desire I would not chose a lover over thee.
And yet my soul is driven for the cause to live to see my Isle of Ireland free.
Thus from her thorny brambles bound a crown, it seems to me on every tree he's seen.
In an unmarked grave they lay you down on May the fourth, nineteen and sixteen.

Five dragons crush the souls within that deathly dank and cold forbidden place.
Two lovers torn from each other's arms, he'll kiss no more the warm tears on her face.
Yet deep within that dragon burned a love, a loyalty so strong to turn history's tide.
To join brothers of that worthy cause and greatly proud to stand at Jesus' side.

FLIGHT

By Anna Brosnan

Your beak is poised,

Eyes set on the Atlantic.

Are you afraid as you balance

In a seeming half-dance,

Your wings in full expanse,

Your flat webbed feet

Hugging that cold and rugged rock

Carved from some eternal dune or cave?

Soon you will be in full flight,

Wings flapping and feathers in ruffle.

Alone, aloof you answer freedom's call

Across ocean waves and mountainous rocks

From home to home without baggage or bite.

Up there you scale the heavens, caress the stars.

Will you kiss the moon for me?

You Gotta Have A Dream, Don't You?

By Bridie Callanan

The Dalai Lama calls "seriousness" an illness. I'm sure the Dalai Lama is right, as sure as I believe I have the cure – now that's saying something.

No matter what we are going through, no matter what we are dealing with, no matter what happens day in and day out, if you cannot find something to laugh about, something to smile about, something to dream about, some way to lighten things up — life can become total drudgery and it was never meant to be like that. You got to have that dream; laugh and smile more. It helps with everything.

I do realize this goes against another of my mottoes, or does it, perhaps in tandem! Live and observe the now, this moment. It may be all there is, so let us try to open our hearts to the fragility of life.

Many years ago someone close to me now long departed said, 'you're in cuckoo land, dreams are for wasters, just get on with things as best you can'.(I do). She may have been correct. We all have to take life as it comes but in the humdrum, the sadness as well as the joy, the unexpected, we surely need a dream, perhaps a little one perhaps an outlandish one, to keep the smile on our face. Some day that dream may/will come true.

I had no choice; it was on my bucket list 'things to do before I depart to a higher plain — see, still dreaming and hoping. I have always wanted to travel, but life got in the way, (in a good way, I hasten to add. (More later!) But my crazy dreams began to come true.

You Gotta Have A Dream, Don't You?

I back-packed with my daughter around South East Asia. I travelled on planes, boat, truck, car, tuk-tuk and bicycle. Overland from Bangkok in Thailand to Singapore, side trip to Siam Reap (Ankor Wat) in Cambodia,

Ever since I can remember I've dreamt of seeing the Great Wall of China and yes, you've guessed! A few years ago on way back from Oz/New Zealand, we took the Beijing route home. I threw snowballs and drank champagne with my husband and some German lads on The Great Wall of China.

I've left my best dream come true until last — my family. Now I'm living it with my adorable grandchildren, the light of my life, unbelievable gifts of joy! Thank God.

My hope and dream now is they continue to be safe, healthy, happy and as strong as they can be and most of all live in peace, but, don't forget to dream a little. My final hope and dream is that all beings throughout our universe, those in pain, loneliness, war zones etc. come to a place of peace, love and freedom, with help of the Almighty God. (It will happen).

'You gotta have a dream, else how're you gonna make a dream come true' I've always tried to have that as my motto and remember it takes the same amount of time and energy to dream of wonderful things as it does to worry, but the results are incredibly different (I'm making this sound very easy and it may be the complete opposite for some, but why not give it a go and do keep trying). God Bless. ☺

MOTHER

By Patricia Horgan

As baby emerged from the womb,
Her mother thanked her god anew.
Each day she watched her rose and crooned
The happy tunes that helped her snooze.
She fed her what is nature's best,
Whilst on her brow sweet kisses pressed.
And as the rosebud opened wide,
She was her strength, her rock her guide
Who walked with her the path of life,
Easing her troubles, sharing her strife,
Who taught her how to kneel in prayer,
To care, to share and to be fair;
And now the rose is full mature,
Nurtured by a mother's love so pure.

FREE WILL

By Anne McCarthy

"Gateway Universal. How may I help you?" A lilting voice answered.

"This is Gabriel. Put me through to Michael please?"

"Gabriel, what's up?" a hearty voice boomed. "I didn't expect to hear from you."

"I'm having a bit of a problem with my client, sir."

"With Tanya?" Michael laughed incredulously. "What did she do? Hurt a fly?"

Gabriel bristled. Michael continued: "Tanya is the sweetest girl. Really Gabriel, if you can't handle Tanya, we'll have to move you back here to headquarters."

"Well Michael, you know that Tanya is perfect in every way, except for one vice – the cigarettes. For her new year's resolution she resolved to stop, and threw all cigarettes in the fire. The craving was tremendous. She tried nicotine patches, chewing gum and exercise, but nothing worked.

After a week of it she couldn't stand it any longer and drove to the local Centra for some cigarettes. She stared at the cigarette machine. I whispered in her ear to resist the urge. She touched her forehead with her fingertips and gently massaged it. Then she slipped a bar of chocolate into her pocket and walked out without paying. Her heart was pumping, adrenaline was racing and for the first time in a week, she wasn't thinking about smoking. Thus began Tanya's addiction to shoplifting."

"What! Tanya a shoplifter! I don't believe it." Michael laughed. "It was probably a once-off thing."

"No. In fact she went home and planned another hoist. Next she lifted Taytos at Tesco's and the day after, a pack of yoghurts from Super Value. Now she is planning a trip to Penny's."

"Isn't she worried about being caught?"

"She's so caught up in the buzz, she's beyond worry. Now Michael you promised me an easy client after the last dodgy one. You told me Tanya was deeply spiritual and always praying to her Guardian Angel. She never makes contact now. I just stand by and watch her mess up. Can't you intervene?" Gabriel pleaded.

"Look Gabriel," Michael reasoned, "you know that Guardian Angels cannot intervene unless her life is in danger. Remember, she has Free Will. I spoke out against Free Will at the time of the Golden Road Agreement but the Union of Humans insisted upon it. We cannot intervene unless the terms of the Agreement are re-negotiated.

Free Will

All you can do is follow her and keep whispering messages of love and peace in her ear. Eventually she might hear you."

Gabriel sighed and hung up. She hung in the mists of despair, her wings trailing forlornly. Michael was right. Giving humans Free Will has been a disaster for the universe. Most humans had no idea how to choose wisely, and created terrible trouble for themselves.

Gabriel's last client was a corrupt County Councillor, who was blind to all her warning messages. He ruthlessly accumulated wealth at the expense of his constituents. Towards the end of his life the media exposed him. He died in shame. When he reached Gateway he refused to cross over into the light and now wanders the world seeking the ruin of souls.

Gabriel's new client Tanya was such a sweet soul. She was married to Ollie who spent most of his life feeling sorry for himself. Tanya took care of him and the children and was always putting a bright smile on everything. Until recently, cigarettes were her only comfort.

Free Will

Michael had had an inspiration. If Tanya went back on the cigarettes her path towards jail could be diverted. Tanya was going to a wedding in a few weeks. What if they organised some Demons to be sent to her house prior to the wedding to stir up trouble between husband and wife? Tanya would go to the wedding upset. Someone would offer her a cigarette and, with one puff, she'd be smoking.

It was a brilliant inspiration, Gabriel agreed. Michael was a superstar among the Angels. She had had a crush on him ever since she joined the Angelic Realm. All the other Angels fancied him. She always held out hope in her heart that one day he would choose her.

The night before the wedding the demons worked on Ollie in his sleep. He spent the night thrashing and turning. He awoke to see Tanya standing at the mirror admiring her stunning rose red dress with matching shoes. Her long dark hair was swept up into a bun and the feathers perched on her hair made her look like a model. Ollie felt a rush of jealousy.

"Is that another new dress you're wearing?" he barked.

"Oh this old thing, I've had it for ages," she lied, quickly hiding the price tag. She made a mental note to be careful about displaying her new acquisitions. Ollie seemed to be getting suspicious of her lately. Only the other day, when she tried out the new make-up she'd taken in Brown Thomas, he accused her of having an affair. Quickly she re-assured him of her love.

He had warmed up somewhat after that. Today, however, he was back in bad form again. She wondered what was eating him. The demons flashed a thought of a lit cigarette; oh, the aroma! Quickly she dismissed the idea.

"Please collect the children from school today and give them their dinner, Ollie," she instructed. "Just re-heat the stew on the stove for them."

"But what if it burns?" Ollie whined.

"Just give it a good stir and don't over-boil the potatoes like you did the last time."

"Well if you're going to be like that," Ollie snapped, "I won't feed them at all."

"Oh stop being such a baby!" Tanya tried to bite her tongue but the words slipped out.

The demons urged him on. "Don't let her talk to you like that. Who does she think she is? Mrs High and Mighty with her flashy red dress and shiny red shoes that she robbed from Brown Thomas."

"Who do you think you are Mrs High and Mighty with your flashy dress and shiny red shoes that you robbed from Brown Thomas," Ollie hissed.

Tanya froze. How did he know? Someone must be watching her. "What did you say Ollie Brown? How dare you accuse me of such a thing? Who told you that lie?" she demanded.

Ollie hung his head. "I have no idea where that came from."

"Oh Ollie, sometimes I weary of your petty moods, Tanya sighed."

Ollie flopped down on the side of the bed.

"What's happening to you Tanya? You were always so sweet and kind but since you've given up the cigarettes you are a different person, like you don't need me anymore."

Tears welled. She dabbed, careful not to ruin her make-up. "Look I must go," she said.

In the car, the Angels sat at the back, while the demons taunted Tanya in the front seat.

"You need a cigarette," they chanted over and over. Tanya switched on the radio. Robbie Williams was singing 'Angel.' Michael smiled in approval. Gabriel beamed. Tanya sang along as she drove. The Angels joined in the chorus. Fresh pink cherry blossoms blew softly onto their path as they drove up to the church.

The Wedding March was beautifully played by the organist. The Bride walked down the aisle holding her father's arm. She looked radiant in the soft light streaming through the stained glass windows. She reached the altar and her husband-to-be took her hand. They gazed into each other's eyes. Tanya felt a stab of remorse over the row she'd had with Ollie.

The demons shuffled in frustration outside the church as they weren't allowed in. It would have been a lovely moment to make Tanya feel sorry for herself over the poor state of her marriage. However, God's house was God's house and they had to adhere to the rules.

When the Bride and Groom left the church, Tanya followed, feeling relaxed and peaceful. The love expressed during the ceremony made her resolve to return to Ollie later and make up. She would work on their marriage and live happily ever after like the bride and groom.

There were four missed calls from home on her phone messages. Quickly she dialled. Jenny, her youngest answered the phone. "What's happening, Jenny?" Tanya asked.

"Daddy's been mean to us. He burned the stew and then he made us eat it. I miss you Mommy and want you to come home NOW."

"Sweetheart, put Daddy on the phone please."

"Ollie, what's going on?" Tanya asked.

"The kids are acting like spoiled brats. It's all your fault! You never trained them properly. They have no respect. I'm sending them to bed: no tea; no computer games. It's time someone stood up to them," he seethed.

"But Ollie, it's only 4 O'clock. Let them go outside and play. It will do you all good."

Ollie hung up. "Cigarette, cigarette," screeched the demons. Gabriel looked on with compassion. The pressure was really on Tanya now.

The wedding party gathered at reception. Smartly dressed waiting staff greeted the guests with crystal flutes of champagne. Tanya gulped her drink like she had just wandered out of the desert. Thoughts of her children were interrupted by the scent of freshly lit cigarettes from the steps. "Just one puff. Just one puff," the demons sang. "What comfort it will bring."

Tanya accepted another glass of champagne and walked over to where a male wedding guest was smoking. "That smells wonderful," she purred.

"Would you like one?" He proffered a freshly opened pack. "I only smoke when I go out socially. It's good for mixing, and meeting beautiful women like you," he flirted.

Tanya noted his amazing blue eyes and white teeth. Even his tie matched her dress. She smiled and took one. The Angelic choir sang 'Hallelujah' as Tanya lit up and inhaled.

"I'm Richie; a pleasure to meet you." He moved closer.

Tanya felt something stirring inside of her.

"Let's have the first dance together tonight," he suggested.

"Mm, I think I'd like that," Tanya murmured as her heart pounded in her chest.

Gabriel rolled her eyes up to heaven. Michael shook his head in dismay.

"Oh no, not Free Will again...."

RAMBLING HOUSE

By Bridie Garvey

Practice the songs and recitations,
Greet the old familiar faces,
Early dancers beat the floor
While *Bean an Tí* cries out *A Stór!*
It soothes the soul - with laughter plenty.
Hurry now,
While seats are empty.

It entertains the lad of nine
Whose granddad Owen is ninety nine.
They swing and sway
To spoons and fiddle,
Bread is splitting on the griddle.
Stories told the age-old way.
So much talent all night long,
Let's have some hush, for one more song.
It's nearly time for Connie's Brushes,
Like a flash he's doing the rushes.
We watch him leap
High in the air
Julia smiles,
Always there.

Rambling House

Goodnight Bean and Paddy Óg,
Mossy Dee and Marianne,
Standing tall
With Music fading
Sadly it's
A great night
Ending.

Amhrán na bhFiann

POETS AND DREAMERS
By James Flynn

Poetry be the twilight journey that takes me to the dawn.
Fashion a smile at the wounded earth
And drift through golden corn.

Poetry be the cheerless scape best seen through a misted pane.
Conferring beauty yet unseen
Upon that which seems plain.

Poetry be the flying gull that soars me high beyond the sea,
To a heavenly space where only poets
And dreamers can feel free.

Poetry be the working men who in concert strike on stone;
Their chime rings out through hill and glen
And beats in measured tone.

Poetry be the dancing pen that leads me God knows where.
Perchance to Paradise we'll stray,
Then Poetry be a prayer.

Tommy Frank O'Connor - Biography

Tommy Frank O'Connor lives in Tralee, Co. Kerry, Ireland.

A novelist, poet, dramatist and story writer, six of his books ranging from Literary Historical Fiction, a Novel for Children, Short Stories and Poetry are published.

His poems, stories and reviews are published in literary presses and anthologies worldwide. Coming from the oral tradition of Irish Bards and Storytellers, his performances have a character beyond mere recitation of the written word.

His work has been performed on RTE Radio and on BBC Radio 4.

He conducts Creative Writing Residencies in Schools, Libraries, Prisons and Colleges. He has served as Writer in Residence for Co. Kerry at various times since 2007.

He assists writers in the production and publication of their work, such as Memoir and Poetry.

He is *Clan File* (Bard) of the O'Connor Kerry Clan.

INDEX

Anna Brosnan – My Favourite Holiday – Page 18, 19

Anna Brosnan – Flight – Page 96

Anne Coffey – Fate – Page 23

Anne Coffey – Journey – Page 85

Ann Kiely – My Favourite Place – Page 42, 43

Ann Kiely – He Looked Into the Blazing Fire – Page 87, 88

Anne McCarthy – The Mission – Page 54, 55, 56

Anne McCarthy – Free Will – Page 100, 101, 102, 103, 104, 105, 106, 107, 108

Bridie Callanan – You Gotta Have a Dream, Don't You? – Page 97, 98

Bridie Callanan – The Summons – Page 63, 64, 65, 66

Bridie Garvey – The Writers Group – Page 9, 10

Bridie Garvey – The Rambling House – Page 109, 110

Cáit Curtin – A Sunny Glade – Page 16, 17

Cáit Curtin – Giving Up – Page 57, 58

Donna McSweeny – Whispers – Page 36, 37

Elsie McDonald – They Lived "The Happy Ever After" Or So They Thought – Page 74, 75, 76

Elsie McDonald – Accidental Adventure – Page 32, 33, 34

Frank Kevins – The Forgotten Boy – Page 13, 14, 15

Frank Kevins – My Favourite Place – Page 69, 70, 71

Fiona Roche – Accident? – Page - 80

Hanna O'Sullivan – Easter – Time for Renewal – Page 21

Helen Blanchfield – Brown Flesk at Night – Page 91

INDEX

Helen Blanchfield – Remembering Julia – Page 80, 81

Helen Blanchfield – Loyalty and Grace – Page 95

Judith Carmody – Woodland Walk – Page 35

Judith Carmody – Petal Wishes – Page 72, 73

Judith Carmody – Angel of Mine – Page 86

Jimmy Cullinane – The Green Grass of Ireland – Page 11, 12

Jimmy Cullinane – Remembering Patrick – Page 38, 39

Jimmy Cullinane – Water – Page 89, 90

James Flynn – Over There in County Clare – Page 20

James Flynn – The Village of Talbots Inch – Page 61, 62

James Flynn – Mount Eagle – Page 84

James Flynn – Poets and Dreamers – Page 111

Lorraine Carey – Funeral – Page 27, 28

Lorraine Carey – My Youngest – Page 67, 68

Lorraine Carey – Deceased in December – Page 77

Madeline O'Connor – The Station – Page 40

Madeline O'Connor – The Wake – Page 83

Madeline O'Connor – The Party – Page 92, 93, 94

Marian Pender – The Reek – Page 26

Marian Pender – October Night – Page 59, 60

Noel Keane – The Spiders Web – Page 22

Noel Keane – The Village – Page 52, 53

INDEX

Patricia Horgan – Flight – Page 24, 25

Patricia Horgan – Bully – Page 31

Patricia Horgan – Mother – Page 99

Patrick O'Connor – Motherhood – Page 44

Rose Riordan – Place – Page 41

Sharon Fitzpatrick – What To Do About ……. Page 29, 30

Sharon Fitzpatrick – Hope – Page 78, 79

Sukie Mac – Dan Got A Chimney – Page 45, 46, 47, 48, 49, 50, 51

Tommy Frank O'Connor – Sliabh Lúachra – Page 7, 8

Tommy Frank O'Connor – Biography – Page 112